# PRAISE FOR

## *An Insider's Guide to Psychotherapy*

"This is the book you give your friend or family member when they're considering starting their own psychotherapy, but they have some questions first. Richard and Kirk have made their wealth of experience wonderfully accessible with these short chapters and the very clear, concise chapter titles. This also would have been invaluable as a new clinician as I was trying to figure out what sort of psychotherapy I wanted to practice."

—JOSEPH HULL, LMSW

"Richard Raubolt and Kirk Brink's *An Insider's Guide to Psychotherapy* is a refreshingly honest, down-to-earth, and solidly grounded resource for anyone seeking to understand the healing power of a truth-seeking, empathically attuned, authentically engaged therapeutic relationship. It is a sophisticated yet remarkably accessible guide to the actual process of psychotherapy. With clarity, humility, and psychodynamic depth, the authors bring to center stage the very questions and compelling concerns that so often prevent people from seeking—or fully engaging in—therapy.

"From common objections to treatment to discerning the hallmarks of good therapy, to thoughtful descriptions of diverse therapeutic modalities, this rich and engaging volume offers readers an informative and empowering road map. It is reader-friendly without being simplistic, clinically rigorous without being doctrinaire or rigid, and broadly relevant for individuals at every stage of their therapeutic journey.

"Perhaps most importantly, Raubolt and Brink illuminate what I consider the heart of deep, embodied healing: therapy as a courageous, cocreated, and mutually impactful exchange—one that invites shared vulnerability, deep honesty, heartfelt engagement, and the possibility of meaningful change when two people dare to bring their true selves into the room in search of what the authors describe as, simply, the *truth*. One way to think about the process is this: The client brings their symptoms, the therapist brings their theory, and—if they are lucky—they both come out of hiding and codiscover the truth.

"At its core, this deeply humane book conveys a fundamental faith in the transformative power of coming to know who you are and finding peace with that discovery. The therapeutic process is not a mystery to be feared but an eye-opening encounter, a profoundly meaningful exchange, to be entered mindfully, bravely, and with hope.

"I warmly recommend this to prospective clients, seasoned therapy participants, and clinicians alike."

—MARTHA STARK, MD, Harvard Medical School, award-winning author of nine books, including *Relentless Hope: The Refusal to Grieve*, on the integration of psychodynamic theory and clinical practice

"My experience of reading *An Insider's Guide to Psychotherapy* is much like the experience I would wish for anyone starting therapy for the first time. As with a good therapist, the reader is welcomed in by the simple and straightforward format of the book. Each chapter states and then skillfully addresses a question common to perspective patients seeking therapy, such as 'Isn't therapy just for first-world problems?' or 'How can I find a good therapist?' The authors deftly articulate the many layers (often unconscious) beneath the original question, educating and gently challenging the reader to deepen their own awareness. The chapters are short yet thorough, setting and maintaining a steady pace throughout the reader's experience. Each chapter, and the book as a whole, is collaborative in tone as is the work of a fine clinician. Drs. Raubolt and Brink ask the reader many questions, inviting a more active engagement in this process of undertaking therapy. The authors, again reminiscent of seasoned therapists, also strike a disarming balance between wisdom and humility; expertise without arrogance. This gem of a book distills the substance and depth of the hard-earned experience of two master clinicians of our time.

"*An Insider's Guide to Psychotherapy* is also a unique resource for practitioners. It is a refreshing reminder of why we became psychotherapists and our ethical duty to continually work on ourselves. Our ability to be fully present and authentic in our relationship with our patient is the crucible of healing and change."

—SHEILA MCCORMACK, PhD

# AN INSIDER'S GUIDE TO PSYCHOTHERAPY

*An Insider's Guide to Psychotherapy*

by Dr. Richard Raubolt and Dr. Kirk Brink



ISBN 979-8-89747-101-0



Cover design by Lauren Sheldon

Published by

köehlerbooks™

3705 Shore Drive
Virginia Beach, VA 23455
800-435-4811
www.koehlerbooks.com

# AN INSIDER'S GUIDE TO PSYCHOTHERAPY

Dr. Richard Raubolt and Dr. Kirk Brink

VIRGINIA BEACH
CAPE CHARLES

## IN MEMORY OF KIRK L. BRINK

My pleasure in seeing the completion of this manuscript is tempered by the gray tones of loss.

Kirk and I worked, played, argued, and collaborated on this, our second book. That only I now have the experience of ushering our words into full fruition saddens me. The unique voice, character, and wit of my coauthor has been silenced.

I received the call on a bitterly cold December morning. Kirk had died—suddenly, inexplicitly. A disciplined man always doing more for his family, patients, and colleagues was gone. With his death, even as he sought health on his trusted elliptical machine, leaves a stale state of emptiness soon to be filled with grief.

Kirk Brink was a force to deal with. He would challenge, provoke, tease, encourage, love, and laugh with confidence and ease. Blessed with a keen mind and insatiable curiosity, he could make room for the unexpected, the unfamiliar. And since *boredom* was a bedeviling experience so unfamiliar to him, he would ban the very word from conversation.

Not all is lost with his death. You can find him in these pages unapologetically living in and through his work. When we first began a writing collaboration, we joked that we might as well, since neither of us planned on retiring. I wish our time together had been longer.

I am reminded of the last lines of the poem "Toads Revisited" by Philip Larkin:

*When the lights come on at four*
*At the end of another year?*
*Give me your arm old toad*
*Help me down Cemetery Road.*

You are missed already, dear Kirk.

**—Dr. Richard Raubolt**

# TABLE OF CONTENTS

# INTRODUCTION

When Kirk was five years old, it became clear to him that something wasn't right with his grandfather. Worries of his life were catching up with him. He was a farmer—never an easy life—and everything was just getting to be too much. So Kirk's grandfather went looking for the only escape he could think of. He went off into the woods, shotgun in hand, ready to take his own life.

Kirk's dad knew what he was up to, so he followed his father, begging him to reconsider. He finally resorted to the only means he had to save his father's life; he knocked him out cold. The grandfather was taken to the hospital and given electroshock treatments.

Once the immediate threat subsided, the grandfather began to meet with a therapist. This was in a conservative farming community in the in the middle of the twentieth century, a time and place when therapy was considered exotic—at best. But Kirk began to hear his father say that there were important changes happening in the grandfather's life, and his father—also a farmer who might have been skeptical of therapy—attributed those changes to what was happening in that therapist's office.

Richard had a much milder, although no less impactful, introduction to therapy. When looking back on his early childhood, he thinks that, even before he went to kindergarten, he began to serve as a kind of therapist for his highly anxious sister. He would soothe her anxiety as a way of taking care of himself. That role suited him well. Years later, another family member developed a drug addiction, and

Richard, familiar with drug-treatment therapies, intervened to make sure effective assistance was provided. A pattern emerged; he could see that therapy helped people.

Two very different and personal introductions to therapy. But each introduction rooted Kirk and Richard in the fundamental belief that therapy, to put it simply, can help a wide range of people meet a wide range of basic needs.

We are Kirk and Richard, and we've written this book because, starting early in life and continuing with decades of professional practice, we've seen therapy do so much good. The world is different now than when we were children. Stigmas attached to psychotherapy have since diminished, but some remain.

Some people think therapists have heads made of putty. They wear beads and sandals and say things that no one understands. Some people think therapists possess magical powers somehow—or want to—and are going to use them to analyze anyone and everyone. We've gotten some measure of delight by telling people at cocktail parties that we're psychologists and then seeing how many people we can get to leave the room. It can be amazingly effective.

Psychology is a suspicious science for many people. Maybe they bash Sigmund Freud because they don't understand him, or maybe they bash him because they do. Either way, they always seem to have him in mind when they consider of our line of work. They have stereotypical images of us sitting in a chair, coldly analyzing people who lie down and pour out their deepest secrets in a vulnerable position, while we analyze them as we look down on them, literally and figuratively. There is both a fascination and a suspicion about the entire process.

Fortunately, the idea of a neutral, aloof therapist has gone by the wayside. When Richard was in graduate school, a fellow student saw a very traditional analyst for about a year, but he never saw the analyst's face after the first appointment. Richard's friend would come in, lie down on the couch, then the therapist would come in and sit behind him. When the session ended, the therapist would get up and leave.

So Richard's friend literally didn't *see* his therapist. Even though we've come a long way from that, sometimes the stereotypes remain.

We led this book, *An Insider's Guide to Psychotherapy*, with our personal experiences because we want to make it clear that most therapists do not go into psychotherapy to control people, to be emotional voyeurs, or to be detached and dispassionate about the suffering of others. When you're ready to seek out a therapist, the first thing you need to know is that whoever you find is probably there for the simple reason that they understand how emotional suffering happens, and they want to help. Therapists want patients to live more complete lives and to be their complete selves rather than what they were trained to be or traumatized to become.

Sometimes patients come to therapists because of some obvious moment of what we call *capital-T Trauma*; sometimes they come because of a change in life circumstances; sometimes they come because something in their life just isn't working. There are no wrong reasons.

And we know that therapy works in many circumstances. Studies on the effectiveness of psychotherapy have found that 75 percent of those who have experienced therapy have found it helpful, and 80 percent were more satisfied with their state of mind than those who had never pursued therapy. Research further demonstrates that psychotherapy is effective for a variety of mental and behavioral health issues spanning a wide spectrum of demographic groups. The average effects of psychotherapy are larger than the effects produced by many medical treatments.

But even if you accept this basic understanding, even if you recognize that therapy can help, you may still have questions or skepticisms, and maybe some concerns are holding you back. You may still have a fear of what might happen in therapy. Most people walk into a therapist's office not knowing how it will go, or how it should go, or what good or bad signs to look for, or whether it's working, or how to know when or whether therapy is finished. It can all be mysterious. That mystery can become a roadblock to seeking help.

That's where *An Insider's Guide to Psychotherapy* comes in. We want to give you a kind of insiders' guidebook to the process. We'll address common concerns about therapy. We'll tell you how to identify what you might need in a therapist. We'll show you how to assess how it's going, and when and why you might need to change things that aren't working. And finally, we'll help you to see how, when, and whether, to bring your time with a therapist to an end—and what should happen afterward.

We've framed this book as a series of answers to questions we've often been asked about therapy. Even if you're not asking these exact questions, each one represents a larger theme that's worth understanding as you work your way through the process. We want to demystify what happens—to remove the stigma and mystery that can keep you from getting the help you need.

One essential point in this user's guide is that there are different kinds of therapists, those specializing in a particular field of psychotherapy, like couples therapy or grief counseling, or those who employ such techniques as meditation for certain types of illnesses. To that end, we have a dozen or so contributing therapists from specialized fields who have written essays contained in the final section of this book. Each of these authors are colleagues of ours who we have worked with individually or in consultation groups. Some of their writings delve into the complexities of psychotherapy and explain the science behind various treatments. Together, these contributors paint a broad and layered spectrum of this field.

We've been therapists for more than four decades and have been patients in therapy ourselves even longer. And, we've also been therapists for therapists, as well for people new to the process. Between us, we have almost a century of experience in this field, and that experience increases exponentially when you roll in the professional longevity of our contributing colleagues. Now, we're ready to be your guides.

Welcome.

# PART ONE

# Common Objections to Therapy

# CHAPTER 1

# Isn't Therapy Just for First-World Problems?

We've heard this one a few times. It's dismissive, so we're tempted to respond dismissively, too:

"Of course it's a First-World problem! What world do you live in? If you're in a First-World existence and have third-world problems, you'd better quickly figure some things out about your life."

We're all familiar with the phrase *First-World* problems. It refers to the kinds of problems we can think about only because we have so many other needs met—food, shelter, jobs, a decent income. It's an acknowledgment of privilege; when we say we're experiencing First-World problems, we're usually sheepish about it. But when we say it in the context of therapy, it's also a way of saying that only after every other need is met should we think about the kinds of things we think about in therapy.

It means something else, too. It means that therapy sounds self-indulgent and provides an indication of confusion about what therapy is. People who say such things believe therapy should somehow only deal with capital-T Trauma or with profound depression and anxiety. If someone isn't experiencing that, then why do they need therapy? If it's not addressing some sort of acute emergency, then isn't therapy self-indulgent?

Anxiety and depression at any level are extremely costly, both individually to the person and socially to family and community. So many of these issues involve with relational problems. If someone is depressed, it's not just the one person; it affects the entire family, a marriage, a community. About a third of Americans suffer from either depression or anxiety. That's indeed problematic, especially if you factor in the ripple effects we're talking about here.

The notion of First-World problems might seem to apply mostly to men, who, in our society, tend to occupy the positions of greatest power and influence. One of the popular characterizations among progressives is that males enjoy a privileged status. And yet book after book after book presents a competing narrative. Regardless of whether they're privileged, men are disproportionately purposeless and adrift. Moving on from traditional definitions of what it means to be male can be confusing for men; they're not quite sure of what to strive for. We see this all the time with kids. Richard has had a number of young adult male patients, and for the most part, they seem lost. They're all too often not as prepared as girls and young women are for elementary school or even college. They don't graduate at the same level. Men are prone to die at a rate three times that of females when it comes to *deaths of despair*—drug addiction or suicide. So this evolution of gender roles, which has really emerged in the so-called *First-World*, has created problems that are not at all self-indulgent to address. Young men disproportionately turn to gun violence to address their feelings. Who among us doesn't wish they had talked to a psychologist first?

We recently came across an amazing statistic. In the early 1990s, 3 percent of men said they did not have a single close friend. A recent poll suggests that has ticked up to 15 percent, which is still surprisingly low. We're becoming increasingly divided, and as a result we're becoming increasingly isolated. And it's costing us. Robert Putnam detailed this phenomenon in his 2000 book, *Bowling Alone*, and since then, thanks in part to the covid pandemic and subsequent lockdown, and to political and cultural divides, things have generally gotten worse. We're not joining anymore, and the resulting isolation is taking a significant toll.

Gabor Maté's book, *The Myth of Normal*, comprises 600 pages of thorough research and clear descriptions of the United States' toxic culture. He argues for the need for therapy (among other things) in the First World. He writes that men in this culture are much more likely to develop addictions, whereas the conditioning for women to never say no, freely and powerfully, is likely related to the high rates of several diseases, including multiple sclerosis and rheumatoid arthritis.

What we address in therapy goes to the heart of anyone's ability to thrive. We know that the highest drive in an infant is attachment. And we know the young child will do whatever it takes, even if it means giving something up, to be attached to a parent. So sometimes that attachment comes at a severe cost to the child. It starts out so soon, and if it goes awry, as it often does, that trauma gets carried for life. That's why people show up in their adulthood with all sorts of difficulties caring for themselves and others, and all sorts of emotional difficulties. And we know that personality is carried across time, place, and situation. So we know that childhood trauma will continue to shape personality and behavior unless people do something to change course. People will make that shift sometimes through a spiritual awakening, through an intervention from family, or other ways. But the most common available way to shift is through therapy.

We've both had patients who had difficulty meeting basic needs—an ability to earn a living, to provide basic security, to be a caring parent or a dependable spouse, because of problems that were being uncovered in therapy. Richard recently had a patient who had finally arrived at the same conclusion his wife had five years earlier—the husband needed help. He had lost a brother in a very difficult situation, a very difficult death, and never grieved. He had traveled to the state where his brother was in the hospital and dying, returned home, and went to work immediately. The two brothers had started a law firm and it was business first. The husband had to get back to work to save the business.

But by just rushing back to work and not grieving, he almost lost his marriage, and his kids, and his practice, the thing he was most focused on saving. He had to work out some of these issues. Simply trying to tuck it away so he could work was actually an ineffective strategy for the work itself, not to mention the repercussions on his family. It's important to understand that, as we develop, powerful systems in the brain activate, and we need to understand what triggers that activation. There can be all sorts of practical implications—problems with rage, problems with responsibility, problems with money. The best way to get to the root of those problems is to understand what happened along the way, so that those who suffer can understand how to make the suffering stop.

Therapy isn't a creation unique to the First World. To some degree, therapy has been around forever. Maybe it involved a fireside chat, or religious teachings, but ultimately all cultures have developed constructive or even therapeutic ways of talking about problems. Sometimes those methods have had downsides if, for example, they became very controlling. But the purpose of these methods of talking with each other help people become free of the handicaps that certain emotions cause. Therapy is more planned and more professionalized; therapists get a lot of training in what to look for. But therapy provides the structure for the change that we've always needed, and that's been there for centuries—regardless of what world we live in.

# CHAPTER 2

# Isn't Therapy Just for "Crazy" People?

*Crazy* is an outdated and offensive term, and provocative. Even in the old days, it depicted *psychosis*—a severe break with reality. It was the sort of thing patients would be hospitalized for because they had become a danger to themselves or others.

But behind this tainted way of characterizing those suffering lies a concern that many potential patients have: Is therapy for people who are sick? Some people worry that the decision to seek therapy means they've crossed some line between mentally healthy and ill, and that just by coming meeting with a therapist they're admitting they have some terrible illness for which they must seek help.

So let us begin to address this concern by letting you in on a little secret: *We've spent lots of time in therapy*. Plenty of therapists have.

And it's not because we're *sick*—or *crazy*. We're entered therapy because it helps us. It helps us as therapists, it helps us in our relationships, it helps us with ourselves.

When Richard told his first supervisor that he was interested in going into therapy, his supervisor referred him to a therapist. Richard saw the therapist, and when he returned, he was livid.

"You could have told me," Richard said to his supervisor. "You didn't have to spare my feelings. You had to let this guy tell me."

"Tell you what?" the supervisor asked.

"I didn't realize I was this sick," Richard replied.

His supervisor didn't understand. "What are you talking about?" he asked.

Richard said, "He wants to see me three times a week."

The supervisor laughed. Finally he looked at Richard and said, "Congratulations. What he was telling you is that you have the ego strength to go deeper, so you could handle three times a week."

That was Richard's introduction to *analytic psychotherapy*. Since then, few people endorse the idea of seeing a therapist three times a week, but the point remains: Going to therapy, and going deep into some set of issues, is not an indication of sickness. It might actually be a sign that you're healthy—and ready to get healthier.

We believe that it is incumbent upon therapists to be in therapy, whether it's continuous or intermittent. The major tool we have through which we conduct therapy is ourselves, and if there are conflicts that are going on in our lives that interfere with our practice we need to address them. We need to identify the behaviors, ways we deal with conflicts, and the origins of our problematic approaches. For example, it is important to know for ourselves whether our own primary way of dealing with our own conflicts is to fight, criticize, withdraw, panic, please, or submit. We all favor one way, or maybe a combination of two, and the important thing here is to know it, be aware of how it developed in us, and have done some of our own personal work to improve our options in responding to conflicts.

Sometimes it's not so much what is happening in our lives as what happens when we're seeing patients. Certain patients can really affect us, and to be effective in our work, at least intermittent therapy can be helpful. In fact, we've written an earlier book, *Therapeutic Group Consultation*, in which we help therapists understand how they can pursue therapy in a group session, which can help them address their own issues as they work through what their patients issues. Undergoing therapy is important work for therapists.

---

We hope we've made it clear by now that you don't have to be *sick* to get therapeutic help. Still, many people might say, "I had a good childhood. I don't really have anything to work through. Why would I need therapy?" There are lots of different ways to answer that question, but for now, let's start with the concept of *trauma*. We talk a lot about trauma, but even the way we talk about it suggests that lots of people don't have any. It's probably more helpful to distinguish between *big-T* and *small-t trauma*.

Big-T trauma might be physical abuse from a parent, or some other horror story. Small-t trauma is much more subtle, but just as powerful and potentially just as limiting. It may take a while for a patient to see this, even though they haven't experienced anything they consider traumatic. Someone who grows up in a very rigid family, for example, in which it was very clear what they were supposed to do and not supposed to do, person might say, "I had a great childhood." Sometimes it's not easy to recognize, but even a safe, stable childhood can be a source of small-t traumas. Yet once patients begin to recognize how confined they remain due to a history of having to master certain behaviors in order to please people in their family, they can begin to understand what's holding them.

Willingness to cross the line into therapy can vary by gender. In our experience, women start coming to therapy earlier; they disproportionately recognize the importance of making relationships work to be successful at whatever they're trying to do. Men tend to come later in life—and when they do, it's usually to *fix* some very specific behavior. That's okay; therapists are familiar with these dynamics. That *fix* can be a gateway to something even more helpful. But if you're only considering therapy because someone else—a spouse or a friend—says you need it, our advice is to wait until *you* know you're ready for it.

A therapist is likely to engage you in a way that would provide an emotional experience that indicates what would be useful. They might ask something like, "What have the last two years of your life been like?

In those last two years, who was present in your life? How long have they been present with you? How do you want to see yourself at the end of your life?" Something to get you talking about what your values are, and then how therapy might fit into that package. Yes, your life may feel fine now when dealing with small-t traumas. But when all is said and done, how do you want to live your life? A therapist may be able to help you address that question.

There might be other motivators for entering therapy. Some people want help in establishing a kind of personal mission statement. They might want to identify their values and how they want to construct their life. Swiss psychiatrist and founder of analytic psychology, Carl Jung, said, "If the path you're on in life has no obstacles, then you're on somebody else's path." An observation like that can jar them out of this mindset that things are going fine—not to complicate their lives, but in the long run to make them better.

And remember, your therapy isn't just for you. Richard has a close friend who's been in therapy for thirty-nine years. When he reflected to this friend that thirty-nine years was a long time to be in therapy, the friend replied, "Yes, but people in my life do so much better when I'm in therapy."

The bottom line is that a therapist won't think you're sick, or crazy, or anything else problematic for coming in to talk. Kirk leads a men's group that sometimes meets in his practice's conference room. One of the group members once said to him, "I bet you see a lot of sick people in here, don't you?" Kirk smiled, gestured out the window, and replied, "No, the sick ones are out there. The healthy ones are the ones who decide to come in here."

# CHAPTER 3

# Don't Therapists Just Want to Talk About My Mother?

Every line of work has stereotypes, and ours is no exception. When *The New Yorker* put together a retrospective of its cartoons about therapy, no topic was more frequently joked about than how much therapists want to talk about mothers.

And there's some truth to the stereotype, of course. We'll get to that in a minute. But first, we'd like to address an underlying concern some people who invoke this stereotype may have.

Many people come to therapy because they have an immediate problem—something that feels acute, rather than chronic. It feels like the psychological version of a cracked tooth or a sprained ankle. They suddenly can't sleep, or they had a blowup at work or at home, or a DUI made them realize they had a problem with addiction. There's an urgency, and they need it fixed as quickly as possible.

In a situation like this, going to someone who may start asking questions about your family history can feel frustrating. We want a diagnosis; we want a plan of treatment to address this change. We want someone to make us feel better as quickly as possible. And a therapist may be able to work this way. Sometimes there really is a faster fix. If you've developed a fear of flying because you saw footage of a plane crash on the news, that may not require a lot of work with a therapist.

But if you have a fear of flying because you were in a plane crash yourself, that's probably going to be a much longer process.

The desire for a quick fix can vary somewhat by gender, as we've discussed earlier. Men are more likely to want to do targeted work to fix a specific problem. Also, busy people may be very task-oriented, with a strong sense of deadlines and a need to see clear progress quickly. But we all want to feel better—the sooner, the better. We don't want anyone slowing down the process. One of those *New Yorker* cartoons depicts patients dressed as armed robbers pulling up to a therapist's office, with one saying to the others, "We get in, we get help, and we get out."

In this context, asking questions about family history may feel like unnecessary and unhelpful. And perhaps, in some cases, it could be. But the field of psychoanalysis has developed with the emphases it has, not because we can't seem to come up with any new ideas or just keep asking the same old questions. Therapists ask the questions they do because so often that eventually those questions get to the root of patients' problems.

---

The single most significant factor in a person's development is the parenting environment that they grew up in. Nothing tops its importance in our emotional and personal development. In all humans, the need for attachment trumps everything. A child will do anything it takes to not have that attachment disrupted. There's often some kind of struggle, because sometimes the parent doesn't like the way the child is trying to attach, for example. In that case, there's a battle in how emotionally free the child can be. This can happen in happy childhoods as well as unhappy ones. So of course a therapist may ask questions about that because there may be important information in your answer about how you're facing your current situation. When you grew up, was somebody available to you emotionally and physically? Was someone attentive to your needs? Was someone consistently available to you?

These aren't simply *deep background* questions; they're part of your toolkit to discern the way you've been trained to respond to life.

There are other questions a therapist may use to guide you through about your past, too, whether they come back to your family of origin or not. Two words that come up especially frequently in therapy are *trauma* and *grief*. There may be a fresh episode of one of these experiences in your recent past, or something may be lingering. Or something more recent might be linked to something longstanding. For example, your grief over a recent loss may be complicated by a trauma from your past that is directly tied to the person you've lost. It can be difficult to grieve a parent who introduced some trauma into your life. And all of that may be complicating your ability to sleep, or stay sober, or hold a job, or remain in a marriage.

These questions about your past are really about where you are now. What we try to emphasize is that therapy goes in two directions simultaneously. One is dealing with the past, which we might call that the *trailing edge*. What has happened? What's been disruptive? What's gone wrong? But if we're only looking to the past, we're missing out on something. We need to move to the *leading edge*. What resources do you have to face your situation? What are your goals? What are your objective strengths? Where are you going? There's a balance in therapy of dealing with the past *as it relates to* who you're trying to be and where you're trying to go.

What we've been saying here speaks to the word *just* in the title of this chapter. Do therapists *just* want to talk about your mother, or your family of origin more generally, or something else from your past? No. They want to unlock something to help you with your problems. This approach may take longer to work than simple cognitive behavioral therapy—identifying thoughts that are not rational and saying they're incorrect. But in our experience, you'll emerge from this longer process better equipped to make sense of how to face challenges not just now, but as new ones arise. Now just a few words about that other phrase in the question: *make me*. We're used to seeing those people from whom we seek treatment, such as physicians, as authority figures. But a therapist can't make you talk about your mother any more than a physician can make you stop smoking. Our job is to help you understand, and to use whatever we believe will work best to help you understand, even as we work to understand.

We're not in Sigmund Freud's Vienna anymore. You don't have to lie on a couch and submit to our authority while we explore tired cliches. But yes, we might still ask about your mother—or your father, or some other authority figure from your childhood. If we do, it's because they might be important to help you understand that recent blowup or breakdown. We want you to understand where you are, how you got here, and how to get where you're trying to go. In other words, we look back to the past so that we can understand the problems we are having in the present and take corrective action in the future.

## CHAPTER 4

# Aren't Therapists in This Just to Work out Their Own Problems?

Therapists have problems too. Everyone does. And it's our job to work on our problems, just as you'd expect your trainer to be in shape, or your doctor not to smoke. You should expect self-awareness from your therapist, and some understanding of how their issues might come into play as they work with you.

But there's more behind the question, obviously. It's in that word *just.* Someone who asks this may really be asking, "Are you working out your own issues at the expense of working on mine? Is this therapy really going to be about my problems, or yours?" Maybe there's a sense that a therapist should have everything figured out before taking on patients—that therapists should be finished, as it were, and not a work in progress. We hope for the same thing from our physicians, too. We want to believe they know absolutely everything about medicine before they come into that room to diagnose and treat us. But the simple fact is that a good therapist, just like a good physician, is always learning—and we should expect nothing less.

How do therapists learn what they need to learn in order to help you? Obviously, it starts with their training in school. They need degrees in specific areas—usually psychology, or psychiatry, or social work, or counseling. Then it's fair to ask what books they've read recently on whatever the subject is. Because many people don't stay up to date on the field—and they should. Continuing education credits can be helpful, but they're not a great indicator of how much a therapist continues to learn; they're a way of satisfying some fairly low requirements laid out by the state. It's probably more important that therapists keep reading, keep attending workshops, keep writing papers, and stay involved in professional organizations. Therapy is a profession that requires commitment; it can't be simply a matter of stringing together some techniques that appear to be interesting.

At his most recent physical, Kirk's physician had him stand on one foot and then stand on the other foot. That was something his physician had learned from his son, who's a neurologist. Before that, he'd simply asked whether Kirk had fallen in the last year; he had asked him the question every year, for years. This physical examination allowed Kirk's physician to *observe*, rather than just ask. He was continuing to learn, and using that learning to help his patients.

The same thing is true for therapists. We need conscientious commitment to understanding new developments in the field, understanding new ideas, applying them where possible. For example, a well-known book, *The Body Keeps the Score,* by Bessel van der Kolk, really changed the way we work with trauma. In school we were trained to talk about traumatic experiences people had, and talk about it again and again and again, hoping that through talking the afflicted would come up with some ways of addressing the trauma and accept the pain it caused. But it wasn't until van der Kolk's work that we began to see that the damage of the trauma happens to the regulatory mechanism in the body, which means that talking about it repeatedly might simply be retraumatizing the person. That was an important development. Therapists need to keep learning, just as physicians do.

Patients want, and deserve, to be the focus of therapy; they want to be the ones being healed. You don't want to feel that you're some sort of laboratory rat being used to solve someone else's problems.

So for a therapist there have to be boundaries. We have several obvious boundaries, which we have learned to follow. One was really overemphasized in our training, and we got to the point where we disagreed with it—and with some of our fellow therapists—namely, that you don't disclose anything about yourself. Now, the boundary was there for this very specific purpose—to keep the therapist out of the treatment. Over time, we found out that that's not such a good rule. Sometimes it's helpful to bring something of a personal nature, but boundaries still have to be maintained. The term developed to try to help us with this, to bridge this gap, is *judicious self-disclosure.* It proffers that a therapist may disclose things about yourself if you believe it will be helpful for the patient. In other words, therapists shouldn't disclose things only to be helpful to themselves. So even with more self-disclosure, we do have boundaries.

As previously stated, we also think it's wise for a therapist to have sought therapy for themselves, to help with their own personal problems. That's why we started participating in and then leading groups of therapists consulting with each other as a good, conscientious way of providing effective, ethical therapy, and to challenge each other. We've been doing that for decades. We believe this is just part of the profession, to be attending to your own strengths as well as some areas that may need further attention. And we think that it's wise for therapists to use their work on themselves as patients—not as a way of treating their own problems—because their experience can be useful for patients, too.

Change needs to keep occurring —for all of us. One of Richard's teachers made the point that for the patient to change, the therapist needs to change. If the therapist is not in the process of changing, if there isn't ongoing development, increased awareness, and working with issues, he or she is not going to be able to take the patient where they need to go. In our model, the relationship between therapist and patient is one of continual, careful exposure—being exposed and exposing each other to novel and hopefully creative situations.

So yes, your therapist is going to be a work in progress—or at least you should hope so.

We think of a Zen quote that feels applicable when considering the mindset we think therapists should have: "Learn until the last breath. Grow until the last moment." Therapists do their best work by continually learning about themselves, about their patients, about new developments in the field. And yes, we would be wise to use all of that to keep ourselves, as therapists and simply as humans, in good mental and emotional health. But that's all finally in the service of helping you be healthy, too.

## CHAPTER 5

# Why Should I Pay Someone to Tell Me What to Do?

If you have this question about therapy, our off-the-cuff answer is simply this: Don't! If you're thinking this way, the odds are that you've got plenty of people in your life already who are telling you what to do. You don't need one more.

If there are people in your life telling you exactly what to do, maybe you've been handicapped by having been taught too often what you should or should not do. Maybe you've gotten used to people telling you what to do. Maybe you've come to depend on it. Maybe you're too often in a position of being a pleaser or of needing that external authority affirming that you've gotten something right, calming your anxiety. So maybe it's become natural for you to seek someone to tell you what to do.

Some people assume that getting help is all about being told what to do or what not to do. We often get that in the doctor's office, for example, we're told to do this exercise, avoid these foods. Experts we trust tell us what to do all the time.

But a person who goes into therapy looking for somebody who will tell them what to do is likely to be disappointed. In fact, if that's your orientation, your therapist may need to talk with you about it, because it might signal the need for a particular kind of help. It may suggest that you're oriented toward being told the right way and wrong way to do everything. That orientation can be a challenge in interpersonal relationships because some people will never be happy with what you do. They may be fostering a sense that you never get it right. They may be undermining your confidence or your ability to make good decisions.

Sometimes, the opposite condition is in play as some people are used to being in charge. Maybe they're an expert in what they do, and they're used to telling other people what to do. Such people are often successful—and busy. They're used to solving specific problems with specific strategies, and they want the same thing from their therapist. They want someone to say, "I can cure anxiety in one session. I can cure that with a phone call." Some people think psychodynamic therapy—trying to understand unconscious processes in a patient's behavior—is unethical, because it takes too long. People don't want to take the time to talk anymore.

With cognitive behavioral therapy, there's this process of seeing thoughts that are not rational as incorrect. So we say, "Stop thinking that!" That may work on the *Bob Newhart Show*, but that's not life. Difficult problems take time. There are no shortcuts. We have been greatly influenced by Martha Stark, who's a psychoanalyst and a very talented therapist. To the question, How long will therapy last? she answers, "It depends on how ambitious we are."

Therapy, if it works well, is experiential. It happens within the room, between the therapist and the patient. We think therapy is most effective, regardless of one's position or status in life, when you can focus on surprise, novelty, that which isn't known, the unexpected. That's where there's a leveling process; that's where a healthier power dynamic emerges, a sense of give and take. There's still a trained expert in the conversation, but now it's two people talking, engaging in a mutual pattern of exploration. We're not going to tell you what to do; we would never be that presumptuous. But what can be discovered within this context could offer surprises to your life—a new perspective, a surprise discovery. Because if there's one characteristic that is common with anxiety, depression, or any more significant disorders, it is this sense that life is too utterly predictable. Therapy should never be that. It should offer a way out.

---

A primary goal of talking with a therapist is self-discovery. What we said in the last chapter may bear repeating here—self-discovery is not self-indulgent. This is about understanding patterns that may be keeping you from living the life you want and need. And in therapy you have somebody who is trained to not just listen to what's said, but what isn't said, and to give feedback about what they hear that the person may not even know they're communicating. It's not simply to learn what we should or shouldn't do. It's to discover what a person wants to do that will be in their best interest—maybe not in the way they learned to think about it when they were growing up, but right now. For anyone to live their best life, they need to understand what they're saying to themselves and to other people. That's a lot of what goes on in the talking in a therapist's office, and in the listening, too.

All of that may sound more complicated than a visit to a doctor's office for a diagnosis. But even that doctor's visit isn't as simple as it may seem. Kirk's physician claims that it's relatively easy to diagnose a medical problem and to prescribe a treatment for it. —The difficult part is getting the patient to follow the treatment. And another challenge is getting the patient to change the behaviors or tendencies that might have led to the medical problem, and what it would take to lead to a healthier life.

According to the Centers for Disease Control and Prevention, 20 to 30 percent of new prescriptions are never filled at the pharmacy and medication is not taken as prescribed 50 percent of the time. For patients prescribed medications for chronic diseases, after six months, the majority take less medication than prescribed or stop the medication altogether.

So, yes, doctors can diagnose a problem and offer a prescription, but sometimes it takes working with a psychologist to do the mental and emotional work required to make that prescription work the way it's supposed to. As it turns out, nothing in life as simple as getting a prescription seems to be.

That's why the discovery of what a person is doing and the search for a healthier way is something that even physicians can't help with as much as people tend to think. How do you help to improve someone's self-discipline? How do you help somebody with teamwork? How do you help somebody be happier? Have more courage? Have more kindness? Have more trust? How to be trustworthy? How to be humble? How to love? How to be loved? There's no medication for these.

So, why not spend your time, your money, and your mental energy to walk into a therapist's office and talk about what's going on in your life? After all, you're paying to talk to an expert. A therapist has training and experience, and follows licensing laws, and is bound to operate within a code of professional ethics.

But maybe the real reason to talk to a therapist is that your best thinking, by yourself or with a friend, got you only as far as you are right now. Are you satisfied with that? If so, that's wonderful; consider yourself fortunate. But if not, how about a fresh look? You've been living with, working at, trying to solve these issues the same way for a long time now. Why don't we work together to try to see your challenges from a different perspective?

CHAPTER 6

# Why Should I Talk to a Stranger?

As children, we were taught not to talk to strangers. We were not supposed to just go opening ourselves up to people we didn't know. If we ignored that advice, we could get hurt.

So when it's time to consider therapy, it may seem strange to pour our hearts out to someone we've never met. If you have good friends, or close family relationships, or a good support network of another sort, you might find yourself asking, "Why should I talk to a stranger about my problems?"

There are often worries behind such a question. Am I betraying my loved ones by talking to a therapist? Shouldn't I rely on the people who really want to help me because they care so much for me? What if, by going to a therapist, I end up thinking differently about those relationships, even to the point of no longer trusting those closest to me?

The title of a previous chapter focused on talking about mothers in the context of a kind of cynicism about therapy. But for patients, talking about their mother can trigger anxiety, too. We want to have faith in our families. We don't want some stranger to undermine those relationships.

Frequently our patients will say, "I don't want to hate my mother. I don't want to hate my family. And if I talk about this, it's just going to end up being difficult to carry on these relationships." To be honest, sometimes that is what ends up happening—but frequently only temporarily. When that happens, it's usually a phase that a patient goes through. You realize certain things about your childhood that cause you to see it differently, and that can, in the short-term, change the way you feel about it. There is room in therapy for all kinds of strong feelings to be expressed and contained, and there's a trained therapist to help you work through it. You may start by expressing anger, but over time, in working with these feelings, more balance develops. You can see the whole of this person with whom you've had this important and complicated relationship. Whereas if you only confide in a friend, that friend might be supportive, but in the process may keep you from seeing the whole picture about your family life, and thus, even while meaning well, may end up keeping you stuck in the same difficult relationships. By having only those close relationships to lean on, you may need someone from the outside to get things unstuck.

There are other benefits to talking with a stranger, too. If someone is foreign to your world, you don't risk comingling relationships, which could mix things up. And there is the opportunity to look at something afresh. In that sense, while we've moved away from an endorsement of pure, objective neutrality in a therapist, we think neutrality is still a valid concept. A therapist should be neither in a close, intimate relationship with a patient, nor in an angry, aggressive relationship. Either stance can complicate relationships. You don't have to manage the history of your relationship with a therapist; you can just say whatever you need to say.

You can risk that because therapists are trained to listen. We're trained in communication, in thinking, in how thinking and feelings interact with each other.

We're trained to listen to what patients say, but also to what they don't say. We're listening for what's unspoken. While humans are busy doing something consciously, quite often, our unconscious is busy undoing it. Therapists home in on those threads, those pieces of information that may be expressed more symbolically than directly.

Also, therapists are trained to be nonjudgmental in how they listen.

We hear hard stories sometimes. A parent might confess to us that they lost control and abused a child. Even if our own moral compass tells us to be outraged, we have to resist *expressing* that outrage. The patient is usually already ashamed, so admonishment does little good, and in fact pushes in the other direction, the way a friend or parent might. They might need to talk about their shame without having someone add to it.

Listening without expressing judgment doesn't mean therapists don't have a clear sense of right and wrong, or don't listen to it. We don't mean to give permission for abusive behavior; far from it! But our job is to understand why it happened, and to help patients understand. That's a crucial step in changing behavior.

---

In therapy, there are also some built-in legal protections for tzhe patient. The therapist agrees to keep everything they hear from the patient confidential, unless they have the patient's permission to share that information, perhaps with a physician or an attorney. There are some exceptions, of course. If the therapist believes the patient is dangerous to themselves or others then the therapist is released from that commitment of confidentiality. We have to decide when we hear about something disturbing, whether we consider a patient's intentions a threat—and we're trained in how to think about that, too. But if you're not currently a threat to yourself or anyone else, your secrets are safe with us—by law. You don't get that kind of legal protection if you're talking to your neighbor across the street. That information given to the therapist is locked up in a vault. Rarely does it come out under any circumstances. That's a hallmark of therapy.

Grief seems like a natural experience for the context of family and friends, rather than a stranger. And yes, those networks are important in the grieving process. But that's also an experience that can be helped by talking with someone who's trained to listen carefully and differently. You might have learned that family and friends only speak positively to minimize the pain or the struggle. You might have learned to be a pleaser in those contexts. Maybe as a child you were told, "Get over it!" So maybe you never learned how to grieve. Those are things that a therapist listens and watches for. We work with grief rather than try to extinguish it. To heal, you have to be able to grieve. Family and friends don't always provide the space for that.

Grief. Terrible mistakes. Difficult relationships. You're not a child anymore. You've got grown-up problems and challenges to work through. It might be time to speak with a stranger.

## CHAPTER 7

# Can't I Just Read a Book or a Website Instead?

It's been a busy time for therapists lately. For whatever reason—whether it's the aftereffects of the pandemic and the lockdown, or the stress of living in a culturally and politically divided world—most of the therapists we know are completely booked up. Couples therapists we refer patients to for relationship crises, for example, now have months-long waiting lists. How do you solve a crisis you're having right now by waiting a few months?

Between the difficulty finding a therapist and the ready sources of information about psychology available now, whether in books or online, people who need help might be tempted to go it alone, to find their own resources to solve their problems. Maybe you're one of them. After all, you're reading a book about therapy right now. Might that be enough?

We think books are valuable, of course, or we wouldn't write one. But our years of practice have convinced us that reading to solve your problems isn't enough. After all, the challenges you're facing aren't simply intellectual. If you're having emotional difficulties you need to do more than simply *understand* what's wrong.

There's a burgeoning field of publishing in self-help books. While there are plenty of smart authors, the genre is still limited. We're almost inclined to say that if you've read one, you've read them all. So many self-help books try to create change through inspiration. The problem is that real and lasting change doesn't come through inspiration; in fact, it doesn't come through the cognitive realm at all. You have to change emotions to change behavior, to change a view of the world. Most self-help books that we're aware of don't attempt that. We even wonder whether they don't discourage people from therapy—not because they deliver so much that no further work is required, but because they promise so much more than a book could deliver and thus may discourage anyone from pursuing lasting change.

Self-help books aren't the only limited answer. Therapy jargon pervades the internet, so sometimes people are using their computers or phones to self-diagnose. There are problems with that, too. One problem is that so much of what is said is not checked by specialists. There's no refereed journal to determine whether what's being said is accurate, and you can find some totally unsubstantiated theories that can actually do more harm than good by confusing matters.

But the biggest problem with self-diagnosis, regardless of the information source you use, is that healing quite simply cannot happen without a *relationship*. It takes a relationship to create change. That's why we think so many therapists are booked up right now. The effects of the covid lockdown and the contentious political and cultural climate have strained and sometimes ended relationships. And they've made it more difficult for us to trust our fellow human beings. We're more isolated than ever. That makes healing especially difficult—and it's keeping more people in therapy for longer.

We know that healing has to occur *with another person.* That's why trying to find healing *in relationship*—group therapy, couples therapy, individual therapy, family therapy—is so important. Healing requires both compassion and firmness. Social media has made it easier than ever before to find communities of support. But who on the internet will tell you the truth when you're fooling yourself, or when you're being manipulative or manipulated? Sometimes that's the most compassionate thing you can do for someone—to let them know when what they're doing or saying is actually making things worse.

We've often said that Alcoholics Anonymous was ahead of its time in developing its twelve steps. Those steps are very similar to therapy in some ways. The first step is, to take it out of specific AA terms, saying out loud, "I have a problem." The second step is saying, "I haven't been able to solve it on my own." Step three is asking, "Will you help me?" You simply can't interact like that on the internet. When you seek your own solutions you're limited not only by purely cognitive understanding, but also by your own processing—the way you handle that information.

---

Of course, we don't want to minimize how useful some developments in the media have been. The pop psychology now saturating our world of information has been useful in some ways. Take for example the scene in the movie *Good Will Hunting* in which Robin Williams, playing the therapist, hugs Matt Damon and says, "It's not your fault," over and over. That's something that has helped a lot of people understand that many of the things they do are related to adaptations made as a child to reduce stress. People have been able to see something of themselves in a character like Matt Damon's. That's a way of understanding some of why you became who you are.

For greater understanding of why you've become who you are, we're going to make reading recommendations that may surprise you. We're not going to point you to self-help books; instead, we think you'll get more from poetry, or novels. They're still no substitute for therapy, but they will bring you deeper into the human condition that's shaping the struggles you may be going through.

We are big believers in reading to keep up with developments in the field of psychiatry. But about ten years ago, Richard went through a phase when he intentionally did not read anything written in his professional language. He switched to novels because they were able to address the human condition in a much more vivid and human way. He was refreshed by the writings of novelists such as Paul Auster and Don DeLillo. They gave him a different language—more imaginary, more visual.

Kirk sometimes recommends *The Divine Comedy*, by Dante. It has a powerful opening line that translates roughly as, "I found myself at the middle of my life on a dark path. I was very afraid, and I couldn't find my way back." What could be a better way into therapy than that? Because then that character has to make the descent into hell—to look at all the dark places in himself.

There are numerous books from across time and cultures that help us examine the dark places in our lives. Most people don't want to venture into their dark side. They're trying to escape it, but by avoiding thinking about it, they often end up stuck in those dark places. The unwillingness to accept the pain of difficult things in our life helps us build a defense for the pain. But the defense then becomes encumbering.

To be in touch with ourselves, to be aware of ourselves, and to be in touch with other people are the most important goals in therapy. Inspiration is a happy thing, but at the end of the day you're going to have to go deeper in order to connect meaningfully with the people around you and really change your life for the better. You're going to need to establish a healing relationship. And while you search for the therapy you need, don't just pick up the latest bestseller on living your best life. Read the good stuff. Prepare yourself to explore the biggest and most important questions we all face.

## CHAPTER 8

# What If Therapy Is Too Expensive?

It's true. Therapy can be expensive.

Some insurance companies will cover therapy, and if you have such insurance that can help. Unfortunately, insurance companies can harm the therapeutic process, too. We are not enrolled with any insurance companies; we're not paneled by any of them. Years ago, Kirk did work with insurance companies, but at that point he was required, after three sessions, to refer patients for psychotropic medication, or the insurance providers wouldn't approve any more sessions. And insurance companies have also sometimes required that they be able to review a therapist's notes in order to continue coverage, which is a breach of confidentiality.

We suggest you ask whoever you do see whether they're covered by insurance and *why* they are covered under an insurance plan. What did they have to do to get covered? What are the consequences for you that they are in an insurance system? Does it affect your therapy? Does it affect the way they do therapy? If a therapist says it doesn't affect their practice, we would be suspicious. Because if it were that simple, why would there be a question? We all want to be as helpful as we can. We know people are struggling financially, so if there were a consequence-free way of offering our services through an insurance provider, we would. It's just never been that simple. Physicians know this all too well. They've had plenty of experience with insurance coverage dictating how they deliver care. We're in the same boat—except that we have even fewer quick fixes available to us than physicians.

It seems nonsensical that insurance companies are permitted to behave this way. States have a system of licensing us. They provide approval of our degrees and experience to practice therapy. Why isn't that enough? Why would an insurance company also have to approve us? Why would an insurance company have to approve of the place you take your car to get it repaired? And why wouldn't it approve of a place you hear has a very good reputation?

So maybe the question of which therapist you can afford, while admittedly grounded in the reality of everyday life, is not just the wrong question to ask, but one that might actually make your problems worse. Maybe it's better to start with some questions that would help identify whether a particular therapist is able to help you. After all, isn't that the way you contact a physician? If you're starting from a point of wondering where the best deal can be found, you may be undervaluing therapy.

Good therapy simply isn't cheap. Few good things are.

But what if you have special circumstances? What if your financial realities are simply too dire? You might be tempted to ask a therapist to work for less money—to cut you a deal. Unfortunately, there are all kinds of problems with that. Any time a therapist reduces a fee, it has to be very closely examined and considered because of the implications both in the present and future. There's a concept Richard learned about when in graduate school called *parameters*, which is making exceptions to your standard way of practice as little as you can each time. So, in other words, you don't make a big adjustment if you can make a small one, because you stay closer to the way you practice that way. Adjusting fees would be one of those things; therapists simply cannot offer the same services for a wide range of prices.

There are exceptions. If we've been seeing a client for a long time, and there's a significant life change—say, a divorce or losing a job—that really does impact their ability to pay, we might reduce fees. That person would have been in therapy for a while and demonstrated a real commitment to the process. They would need to be invested in the work and we invested in them. But without such specific circumstances, making individual adjustments to fees can be confusing to the patient. How could it not be? If you're going through the grocery line, and they say, "We're going to reduce the cost of *your* groceries." That might be perceived as a random and arbitrary way to run a business.

You might wonder whether you could see a therapist, say, only every other week rather than every week. We strongly prefer not to work with someone every other week unless there's some clinical reason. Every other week doesn't mean they get half the treatment; they get more like 25 percent. It doesn't simply cut the treatment effectiveness in half; it affects the intimacy that gets developed; it affects the momentum that gets developed, which can mean therapy ends up taking longer anyway.

If you're worried that therapy might be too expensive over a longer period, you could try starting with a more targeted approach. If you have a particular concern, you might focus on that as you get comfortable with therapy and find out whether it's really something for you to pursue. It's common for patients to come to us for very specific reasons. Very, very few patients come to treatment saying, "I want the long-term treatment. Let's do this for years!" And yet those first few weeks can help you get comfortable with the process and help you see the real value of therapy. Once you see that value, you can reevaluate how to make choices to be sure you get the help you need.

Regardless of the path you take or the length of time you're in it, therapy costs money. But what if not getting therapy ends up costing more?

Therapy can address the many issues surrounding money: The ability to find and hold a job; to do well enough at the job to get a promotion or a raise; the ability to manage money; damagingly expensive lifestyles. How much might someone be spending on alcohol? On marijuana? On cigarettes? How much money are they spending on things that really interfere with their life? And there are other costs to address, too. What might it be costing someone to not have a supportive social group because of the emotional difficulties they have that keep them out of forming good relationships, or difficulties staying in a healthy marriage? The list can go on and on.

So if you're counting costs, be sure to count the costs of *not* getting therapy. And then turn the question around: Given the benefits of understanding how to live a better life, might this be some of the most important money you'll ever spend?

# CHAPTER 9

# What's Really Going on with Me?

Up until now, we've been answering a lot of skeptical questions about therapy. If you're inclined to ask those questions, you're not the only one. We hear such questions frequently.

But here we're going to draw on our experience of therapy—both as patients and as therapists—to address the feelings that often drive such skepticism. Yes, we know, that's just what a therapist stereotypically would say, "You asked me a different question, but here's what's really going on with you." But we've been doing this a long time, and those years of experience have shown us that there's usually something deep-seated that keeps people away from the therapist's door. Therapy is a serious undertaking, and sometimes those skeptical questions are there to shield bigger, deeper concerns that underly them.

The decision to seek therapy usually comes after a period of wondering about it. That can be a winding path. Very few people just wake up one morning and think, "I should find a therapist." Maybe there's a life event that triggers that wondering, some big shift that reveals some sort of stress, or disappointment, or grief, or simply a change in your life's path. Maybe a friend keeps encouraging you to see a therapist. Maybe you've long felt like it would be good to talk to someone about something you've noticed in yourself. But at the same time, maybe you've never had therapy, so it feels like an unfamiliar transition point. And that can expose a range of internal worries and roadblocks.

We should know. We've both been in therapy, and what we encountered in ourselves as we approached it was challenging. For one of us, it took decades to overcome. So if you've facing deeper fears about therapy, join the club. We've been there. Maybe it will help to read about what we went through to get to the point of being ready for therapy.

---

Kirk became interested in therapy at an early age. He saw it help his grandfather; he really enjoyed a class taught by the school psychologist in the eighth grade. The next year, he had to pick a career to research and report on, and he picked psychology. But he never made an appointment; he kept his interest strictly academic.

At the same time, he was suffering from what he would now call anxiety. But he didn't make the connection. He assumed that everyone experienced what he was going through, and he didn't want to talk to anyone about it.

He wasn't required to be in therapy in his training to become a psychologist. But he eventually became increasingly exposed to people who had been in therapy. He realized he was attracted to qualities many of them had. They were clearly in contact with themselves and made good contact with others. They were emotionally grounded and expressive, confident, playful, caring, and curious. They were open and non-defensive, yet reasonably protective of their boundaries. They appeared to have a full personal and interpersonal life. He began to want what they had.

But he still wasn't ready. Kirk convinced himself that what they had was a product of age and experience, and that, as he grew older and more experienced, he would naturally become more like these people he admired. He now sees this as self-deceit, but he wasn't aware of it at the time. He couldn't yet see—or admit—that therapy would help him.

Looking back, Kirk can now see his fear of vulnerability and all the ways he deceived himself and resisted asking for help would later form the core work of his therapy. Sigmund and Anna Freud identified eight such ways we deceive ourselves and called them *ego defense mechanisms.* They include things like rationalization, denial, and projection, among others. Kirk had learned them cognitively; he still needed to learn them emotionally. And he was relieved, after many bumps in the road, when he finally found himself in the right therapeutic relationship to begin to get to work.

Richard was also anxious as a child, though didn't know this was the name for what he was suffering. Unfortunately, those who raised him didn't, either. His father followed a classic World War II playbook. He had earned recognition as a pilot during the war, returned home, established a successful law practice, and became a respected community leader. And he thought Richard could achieve anything with discipline, religion, and hard work. He held himself out as the example for such success.

Richard's dad wanted him to follow in his footsteps and become a lawyer, but Richard wasn't interested; he wasn't sure he was smart enough and charismatic enough to follow his dad. That became a nagging theme for Richard—a fear of simply not being good enough, of being discovered, sooner or later, to be a fraud. He was labeled as having potential, which felt like code for not being as good as he was supposed to be. It was just a matter of time, he thought, before everyone figured out the truth.

In his family, psychotherapy was considered treatment for the severely disturbed. He heard his father refer to a psychiatric hospital as the "nut house." What was curious and most disheartening, though, was the failure to inquire about Richard's thoughts and emotions in general, and when he was struggling. Despite his mother's reverence for American pediatrician Benjamin Spock, who advised parents to be more nurturing, Richard was instructed to study harder, stop worrying, be patient, pray more often, and forget about any setbacks as quickly as possible. His displays of emotion, especially anxiety or tears, were considered signs of weakness.

Despite all this, or perhaps because of it, Richard eventually settled on counseling as a career. He had discovered by then that people sought him out to talk to about their problems, and he enjoyed helping them. Yet even as he was settling on therapy as a career, and even as he continued to battle periods of acute anxiety, like Kirk, he still wasn't sure therapy was right for him. He thought he could solve his problems by working hard and being useful to others. And he was still afraid, deep down, that if he went to therapy he would be told that his problems weren't solvable, that in fact they could be traced back to a single haunting problem—he just wasn't all that smart. That was, he was convinced, his fatal flaw. And he was succeeding as a graduate student in psychology in an Ivy League institution.

His first professional position as a therapist was in a drug-treatment program where he was supervised by a psychiatrist who quickly recognized Richard could benefit from therapy. Despite Richard's attempts at evasion, he would patiently challenge his excuses of not having enough money, time, reliable transportation, or any idea of whom to see. Fortunately, he wouldn't buy the delaying tactics. And eventually Richard found the first of several therapists who have been able to help him over the years.

Fear of vulnerability. Fear of being found out as a fraud. Self-deception. A whole range of anxieties. A deep sense that therapy is for other people. There are only two of us, so there are only two first-person stories here. Your story may contain elements of ours, or something completely different may be involved. But regardless, even the real reason you've stayed away is probably not concern about paying someone to tell you what to do, or the fear of talking to strangers. It may be some deeply rooted struggle that touches on any of the concerns we discuss here—or none of them. But whatever it is, we believe that when you finally summon the courage to walk through that door and meet with a therapist, and you're asked, "So why are you here?" you'll experience the relief that comes from beginning to give an answer.

# PART TWO

# Getting the Help You Need

## CHAPTER 10

# How Do I Find a Good Therapist?

Deciding to seek a therapist—and find one— can feel overwhelming. But it's worth the effort. Good therapy can be a life-changing experience that brings a level of clarity and understanding in your life that you've never had before. So how do you get started?

In such situations, most people start by searching the internet. There's helpful information there, but some unhelpful information, too. Well-meaning people on social media, for example, will tell you how to take charge of the situation, to conduct a kind of interview with a therapist. The goal appears to be to empower people to be in charge of their therapy. But they end up advising them to start with an excessively critical interview oriented entirely to the patient's wants without considering that a trained professional may be able to see some things that they don't see. For instance, say somebody wants help strictly with clearing up some sort of addiction. Addictions can come in many different forms, and usually at their heart is a fear of dependency. Patients don't necessarily see that—and they don't see that if fear of dependency is a core issue, there may be deeper problems to be addressed.

So while it's important to be able to question what a therapist has to offer, and to clearly state your needs, that happens best as part of a thoughtful discussion in therapy, rather than a knee-jerk reaction going in. It's okay to be nervous about getting into therapy, but at some point you'll need to think through that distrust and begin to overcome it. Without that, therapy won't work. Ultimately, you'll develop a feel for how and whether to trust your therapist as you move forward.

One way to overcome your concerns about choosing a therapist is to seek a referral from someone. It could be a physician, a clergy, or an attorney, particularly someone in family law. It could be somebody who has had a successful experience in therapy; they might well give you the name of the therapist they saw. Such a person will also be unlikely to see any stigma to seeking therapy, which may also help ease your concerns. So that's a good starting point.

Then, particularly if it's a friend or colleague who gives you the referral, you should ask about their experience with this therapist. If they're willing to talk about it, ask if they were anxious, when they ran into a difficulty, or when they had a crisis. Therapy is going to be different for each person, but there is a general sense of how the therapist is likely to be able to handle conflict, or discussions about medical conditions, or whether there are certain things that are out of bounds right from the start.

And yes, you should ask questions of the therapist. Pay attention to some degree to their answers, but more to *how* they answer. Do they get defensive? Do they welcome the questions? Don't keep the questions coming rapid fire; give the therapist a chance to respond and observe their response. It's not a good sign if they're threatened by questions. Now, they may choose not to answer some questions for good reasons, or they may say that they'll answer a question at a later point. Sometimes when the question is of a more personal nature, we might say, "I will answer your question, but I'd like to take three or four weeks, and if it's still an important question, I'll answer it directly. But let's explore why you're asking that question." That could look like an avoidance, but it really is an attempt to try to help them get at what's behind the question.

As you observe how they respond to your questions, notice your own reaction, too. How comfortable do you feel with this person? How genuine do their answers seem? If you come into the room anxious, does that anxiety increase as the meeting with the therapist goes on, or does it diminish?

What kinds of questions should you ask? There are some basics, of course. How is payment handled? Is there a charge for missed sessions? How soon do you have to cancel before being charged? How does the therapist handle emergency phone calls, or any other communication between sessions? And then there are some bigger questions: What if you disagree with the therapist? How are those conflicts resolved?

Your therapist will ask you about what's brought you to the point of seeking therapy. That, as we've said earlier, will usually be a specific trigger—a particular moment or episode in your life. But you can be upfront about whether you're expecting treatment for a specific problem, and if so, what their experience is in dealing with such problems. Again, notice how they answer the questions as well as the substance of what they say. Notice how it feels in your body as they respond. Do they put you at ease or make you feel defensive? Do they seem too forward or too familiar too quickly? Do they seem aloof? These are all perfectly legitimate queries.

Kirk will usually tell patients that at least by the third meeting he will try to define what he deems their problems and what he thinks is a way to approach them, a sort of a treatment. That demonstrates to the patient what Kirk is thinking about. Usually, on that third session, he will also ask how he has disappointed or let them down. This provides useful information but, maybe more importantly, encourages honesty. And he'll also say, it's time to decide about whether they'd like to continue—and he decides to continue also. That kind of mutuality can be helpful in establishing a common ground of trust.

Richard is in the habit of asking, at the end of an initial session, how a patient experienced him.

Whatever they tell him, he's going to ask for the other side of it. If they're complimentary and feel comfortable with him, he'll tell them he appreciates that. But then he asks them to tell him something that may have given them pause, or that they wonder about. Not every therapist will do this, but that's the kind of leveling engagement that we think is important to get therapy off on the right foot.

Even if really getting into the heart of what you've come for doesn't start right away, therapy begins in that first session—or even in the phone call you made to reach out to a therapist even before that first meeting. Because giving you the help you need is rooted in relationship. And it's important to see how that relationship feels *to you* from the very beginning.

# CHAPTER 11

# What Can I Realistically Expect out of Therapy?

We've written earlier about those skeptics on social media who encourage you to go into therapy with your guard up, on the offensive, ready to take charge. But skepticism is far from the only attitude you're likely to have encountered about therapy. You might have also come across what we might call evangelists for therapy. They might be therapists, or they might be patients. But if you've been around people who talk about therapy, there's a good chance you've encountered an evangelist.

We are, of course, firm believers in what good therapy can do. But at the same time, we won't line up behind the evangelists and shout "Amen," either. Because they often promise something that therapy cannot, on its own, deliver.

What do we mean by *evangelist*? Well, we choose that word deliberately for its religious connotations. A therapy evangelist is someone who believes that therapy is a solution for everything. They are likely to have the zeal of a convert. Maybe they were once therapy skeptics, or maybe they came from a family where no one was in therapy, and their own therapy suddenly changed the way they saw everything in their lives. Suddenly, everyone they know should be in therapy. It's not enough that their lives have been changed for the better—now yours must be, too.

For such people, unfortunately, therapy can become almost a new identity, which is a problem for a field that strives to help people find their own identity, rather than someone else's. If you hear several times in a conversation, "My therapist says," you might reasonably wonder if they've begun to swap their own identity, their own self, to become a kind of therapy disciple.

Unfortunately, some therapists encourage this way of identifying with what they say; they promote a kind of discipleship. We sometimes refer to them as *messianic* therapists. They tend to develop answers to more and more questions. Maybe they began their careers by offering traditional therapy and over time developed particular angles regarding diet, or various unusual practices that they and their patients swear by. Over time they can move from the mainstream of accepted therapies and begin to do something dramatically novel.

Chuck Dederich is one example. In 1958 he founded the Synanon Institute in California, and he developed the Encounter Game. It really caught on. He used therapy, with his charisma and growing power, and took people under his wing. The Encounter Game looked like a form of group therapy, and in fact it began to be widely used by those with drug addictions But it became apparent that this was a kind of *attack therapy* became both manipulative and harmful. Dederich preached addictions could be conquered through self-reliance and taking responsibility for one's actions. Dederich's charisma and very specific, concrete answers to everything, appealed in a therapy setting to those lost, who had tried traditional therapies, and were prepared to move to the margins of accepted approaches.

Synanon is an extreme example, but less extreme versions of this pattern seem to be on the rise again. Maybe the therapists have traditional training, but for whatever reason they become skeptical of the usual practices with the time-tested boundaries, and they begin to experiment—and they really begin to believe in their experiment. And all too often that combination of certainty, novelty, and charisma ends up attracting true believers.

These new forms of therapies almost seen like fad diets. They offer something new, require total devotion, and they promise total transformation. These therapies can go beyond fads—especially in a group context—and morph into full-blown cults. This search beyond traditional boundaries seems to be dovetailing with a broader movement of skepticism regarding the *establishment*, in fields ranging from healthcare to psychotherapy, and even into politics. Whatever combination of factors have gone into this general dissatisfaction, it seems to be creating true believers in all sorts of movements, including therapy in general and very particular sorts of therapies.

And there seems to be a search for authority, too. Sometimes we'll have new patients come in and say, "I wanted to work with you because I heard you're the best around." Maybe we should be flattered by this, but instead it raises our awareness of something that may need to be addressed in therapy. It usually means that they're looking for an authority figure to submit to, and they're looking to someone who can offer them total transformation. Often people who are susceptible to the search for this sort of all-encompassing reorientation are looking for answers, which means they can be put off by questions. So when we respond by asking lots of questions, they can become disillusioned and move on to someone else.

We've seen a pattern emerge in recent years of spouses or partners insisting not just that their significant other go into therapy, but that they go into a very particular sort of therapy, maybe with a particular sort of therapist. Kirk has seen this in his practice: Five different spouses, who couldn't possibly know each other or even move in the same social circles, had latched on to a new kind of therapy and insisted that their spouses get into it. Maybe they heard about in on a podcast, saw something on Facebook, or they heard someone's testimony about it. Whatever the reason, they thought this new approach was everything they needed. This seems like a destructive use of therapy, but it can be difficult to break through that quest for certainty.

---

This gets to the heart of what we believe you could reasonably expect from therapy. Long before answers emerge, you should expect questions—lots of them. Good therapy isn't one size fits all. It is best when tailored to your unique situation. And your therapist should be able to draw on lots of streams of thought. In our practices we rely on what we learned in school, but we also read fiction, philosophy, and wisdom literature. An effective therapist will listen before they start delivering pronouncements, and to have to think carefully about your background and context. Your therapy shouldn't look like a mass movement. Good therapy, after all, is always retail, never wholesale.

If you're encountering an evangelist who insists that you need therapy, it should prompt genuine reflection for you. Do *you* see the need, or are you feeling forced into it? Because if you're being pressured and you're just going along, the odds are that the therapy will be ineffective. For therapy to succeed, you would do well to make it your own—and your therapist would, too. Be prepared to ask questions and to be asked questions. Good therapy is *co-created*, as we've said elsewhere. Hope for, and expect, good surprises that are unique to your situation.

If you feel the need for someone to take charge, it would be wise to talk about that with your therapist. But don't ask your therapist to take charge or go along if it seems like that's their approach. Therapy is no place for messiahs, or disciples, or one size fits all, or for the big new thing that will answer every question and solve every problem. Instead it's for the hard, messy, and ultimately rewarding work of finding your own way in the world.

# CHAPTER 12

# Could I Just Take Medication Instead?

Maybe. Or maybe not. How's that for an answer? Medication isn't always the solution, but it can be in some cases, or at least part of the solution.

Sometimes patients come to us explicitly seeking an alternative to medication. Everyone is telling them they should take meds, but they don't want to, so they try talk-therapy as a means of avoiding medication. They worry about the side effects of pharmaceuticals, or they worry about addiction, so they'll try anything else first. And of course many therapists like us cannot prescribe drugs because we are psychologists, *not psychiatrists*, who are medical doctors.

Sometimes a patient hasn't thought about medication, and it may be clear to us that it would be very helpful, in which case we might bring it up. We might end up talking to the family physician and make a suggestion. Family physicians often appreciate suggestions for what they might prescribe, because they might think medication would be helpful but not be sure where to start. They're often relieved to know the person they're prescribing the medication for is going to be talking to us. So, if something does come up, either we'll call the physician or encourage the patient to call the physician. It can be a good tag-team approach to the need for medication.

Among the most prescribed medications for relieving anxiety

is Xanax. But there's an important downside—it can be addictive. Anyone with a history of substance addiction must be extremely careful with Xanax. And of course, you don't have to have a history to develop an addiction. There are other reasons to be careful with it, too: Long-term usage seems to increase the odds of cognitive decline, for example. But in general, we see the people who need an anti-anxiety medication like Xanax take it too little, rather than too often. Sometimes the risk of addiction scares people into avoiding a medication, even if it is needed.

For example, you might have to fly, and flying may cause panic attacks. We think you should talk to a therapist about why flying induces panic attacks and how to think differently about it, so that in the long run you're able to take control of that panic. But that doesn't happen quickly or easily. Meanwhile a panic attack can be a powerful and damaging force. Anti-anxiety medication can work in twenty minutes—sometimes less, simply because you know relief is coming—and sometimes you simply have to make that feeling subside. In those cases, Xanax can be a good short-term solution. The long-term fix comes with talking with a therapist about the anxiety so that you'll have the tools to fight off that feeling without introducing the possibility of substance abuse.

---

There are certainly situations in which, as much as we champion the benefits of talk-therapy, we see a need for medication. Panic is one such situation. Depression can be another one.

A revolutionary class of medications that have emerged in the last forty years or so is selective serotonin reuptake inhibitors, or SSRIs. They work with the way that the serotonin in the brain communicates at the level of neural synapses. People report after taking an SSRI that they have better memory and are better able to concentrate. And that gets to the heart of what was contributing to the depression: They couldn't rely on their brain in the same way. So once they get on an SSRI that's effective, depression is reduced because the of the brain's restored abilities. Patients can concentrate; their short-term memory is restored. Although they're called antidepressants, they work with the *mood of depression* less than they work with restoring optimal brain activity.

There are other approaches that help to restore that brain function and thus fight depression. We know with depression, for example, that research has shown that physical exercise can be powerful. But for it to work, you have to take specific steps, repeatedly, for a certain amount of time, just about every day. You must raise your heart rate and your body temperature for at least half an hour through moderately strenuous exercise. It requires tremendous self-discipline to exercise every day and it can take twelve weeks to see any effect. By the time you get to a therapist, you may already be in a such a depressed state that it seems unlikely that anything will work; or you may be struggling with self-discipline. So while exercise may be just as effective, it may be difficult to follow through. For those reasons, taking a pill every day may be more effective for you. SSRIs can be highly effective, which seems to present some patients with a problem. They fear never being able to get off the medication. And yes, the side effects can be difficult to live with. But SSRIs aren't habit forming. The fear of not being able to get off them is rooted in just how effective they are. Patients may feel conflicted by side effects they find unpleasant and the fact that the medication is working.

You might expect that, as talk therapists, we would have a bias against medication. We don't. We've seen how effective it can be. Our main concern is that we have seen it prescribed *indiscriminately*. Some physicians, and even psychiatrists, have failed to distinguish between sadness, grief, and depression. Anyone who prescribes medications to counteract grief, for example, isn't using them for what they were designed.

If your depression is not of a biochemical nature, you may get greater benefit from talk-therapy. This depression is a shutting down—a *depressing* of feelings. What's contributing to that? How long has that been going on?

Often it starts very early. Maybe the best way to please your parents was to not have strong feelings. That can become a pattern, a way of managing emotions. It's not healthy, either emotionally or physically. Shutting down emotionally can even have an impact on a person's immune system. Once patients learn this, once they see that this pattern is keeping them from good health, or from accessing their emotional life, or from being the partner they need to be, they begin to make changes. Therapy can help with the diagnosis—and the cure.

Bessel van der Kolk, in his groundbreaking book *The Body Keeps the Score,* recommends a variety of approaches, including mindfulness practices, psychotherapy, and medication. You might need all three, or one or two might prove particularly helpful. In our practice, we try to assess the kinds of treatment that would be most helpful for each patient. We tell them to pay attention to diet, exercise, and sleep patterns, as well as ways of thinking. Talk-therapy is what we do, but in our assessment that may be only a small piece of what we advise. So it is best not to rule out medication—but maybe also not the best place to start, either. Make sure your therapist knows and explores the full range of tools that might be available to you.

## CHAPTER 13

# Should I Meet with My Therapist Remotely, or in Person?

During the covid pandemic, we all became acquainted with remote meetings. Whether for school, or for work, or simply for seeing friends and family, we found a lifeline by talking to each other through our computers. It was helpful, but it was often frustrating, too. Therapists had the same experience. There were gains and losses in the move to seeing people online. You might have a similar reaction if you end up in therapy remotely, which is more likely than ever before.

Obviously, there are differences between seeing your therapist remotely and going to their office. With an office visit you go through a ritual that can be a way of preparing yourself for the ensuing conversation. You make the commute; you sit in the waiting room; you enter a space that you're only in for that one purpose. You see your therapist in three dimensions—and you're seen in three dimensions, too. You are physically present in the same space in a way that feels important, which we felt acutely as the lockdown ended and we returned more and more to older patterns. We took these experiences for granted before; now we all notice the difference. We don't experience that encounter in the same way remotely.

On the other hand, when you see your therapist from home, you're more likely to be in a comfortable space, though obviously there are circumstances in which that isn't true. It's an efficient way to meet since there's no commute. It might feel less threatening to be in a familiar space, so you might be more at ease and, therefore, be able to open up more quickly.

As therapists, we have different data when a session is in person versus remote. The two of us usually prefer in-person therapy, at least at the beginning of a therapeutic relationship. We feel much more comfortable in person because we can pay more careful attention to a full range of things, from facial expressions to the movement in the room. We can see the whole body. And it frees us up to be more active in our responses. We can try different things that we can't do as easily remotely.

And of course there are logistical challenges with doing therapy remotely. Therapists need to have access to multiple platforms, in case any one of them proves faulty, such as poor internet service. It can be really unsettling to reach a breakthrough or have some other kind of important moment only to realize that the screen has frozen, and the other person didn't hear what you just said. Few things can disrupt the intimacy of a therapy session faster than a technological glitch.

Still, there's a lot for us to work with through that computer screen. Kirk, for example, has been trained in neurolinguistic programming, so he can learn a lot simply by focusing on what's happening on a person's face. We know if we ask a person what they're feeling, their eyes have to go down, or they won't be in touch with the feeling. That's the way the brain works. If we ask someone to spell a difficult word, their eyes will move around, because they're framing the word visually to spell it. If a person needs to argue, they want to use the left hemisphere of their brain, so we might have them look to the right to make their argument so that they have more contact with their left hemisphere. If they're going to make an emotional statement, it's the opposite. That's the right hemisphere, so they look to the left. They tend to look up when accessing the creative part of their brain. So since we know there are things that people do automatically, we can sometimes read those much more easily on a screen, since there's less for us to pay attention to. There can be important clues for a therapist in a session with more than one person, too. With couples in marriage counseling, for example, it's diagnostically significant if they're in the same house and they're using two different monitors rather than one—or one rather than two.

There are other things a therapist can learn from seeing a patient or patients in their home. How neat is the home? How much noise is there around? Are kids running back and forth? If a child comes onscreen, how do they respond to that? Do they push them away?

During the covid lockdown, some of that data became especially important; it spoke to the circumstances of their daily lives under that constant stress. It's important to know what kind of access patients have to privacy, for example. A therapist can get a real sense for that online.

---

Being online and being in person are really two different forms of the kind of intimacy required for good therapy. Since we've been able to be present in person with others after the lockdown, we've been reminded that in some ways there's no substitute for being in the same room with other people. But at the same time, when we meet virtually, we're usually looking directly at each other, with faces that can be larger than life, in a way that can feel even more intimate.

Is one approach better than the other? There is no one-size-fits-all answer. We have observed that people who are most comfortable with virtual therapy are likely to be more self-contained. On the other hand, those who insist on doing in-person therapy may feel more connected and engaged, enabling them to garner where they stand with their therapist. When doing therapy online, they can't read the therapist's body language and figure out what might be going on, and that makes them nervous.

Given that it's possible to have strong preferences about therapy sessions in person or online, you might think that it would be good to be able to honor those preferences and choose the one that makes you most comfortable. But that's not necessarily the case. It may be that if you have a strong preference for one over the other, that preference should be investigated. If one approach makes you nervous, that too is data that needs to be factored into your treatment. Your therapist may need to find a way to make it safe, or at least safe enough, to try something that unsettles you.

The important thing to look for in a therapist regarding this question is whether they're putting your needs ahead of their convenience. It is their job to do their best to understand what you need—even more than what you want. Fortunately, we have more tools available than ever before to figure out just what that might be.

# CHAPTER 14

# Who's in Charge Here, the Patient or the Therapist?

As we said earlier, there may be an immediate need to understand the nature of the relationship between patient and therapist, and in particular, to establish the nature of the authority each person brings. After all, the therapist is the expert, but it's the patient's lived experience, not the therapist's, that's at the heart of the conversation. So, who's in charge?

We mentioned in the previous chapter the growing body of social media influencers who tell you to take charge of your therapy. They're tapping into a particular fear patients may have and offering something that feels like empowerment. But that form of felt empowerment may actually make your therapy longer and more difficult if you're not careful; it can leave walls up between you and your therapist that will require more time and effort to take down.

If, for example, you go to a physician with some sort of pain, you expect the physician to accurately diagnose what's wrong, prescribe a treatment and help you feel better. They went to medical school for this, so they're the expert, and you want to be able to trust them. But a therapeutic relationship is different; while the therapist has expertise, what needs to be uncovered in therapy is usually more complex than a common physical ailment, and the healing process can require a greater level of understanding and participation from the patient than, say, fixing a broken ankle. Therapy needs to be a more collaborative process.

Let's begin by saying that we often encounter one of two very different sets of expectations—patients who resist any sort of imposition of authority, and patients who practically beg for that authority. We might loosely categorize the former as *fear of engulfment*, and the latter as almost a *desire for engulfment*. Both present challenges for a healthy relationship with a therapist.

We believe that good therapy is co-defined. It is two people in charge. It's the therapist and the patient. And we usually say as much. This is not going to be a situation in which we simply will define what's going to happen, and how it's going to happen. There should always be a back and forth. We might pursue something and then stop for a minute and say, "How was that? Was it helpful? What was not helpful about it?"

When we say that authority is *co-defined* in a therapeutic relationship, we need to stop and say that that's not necessarily how we were trained. We were trained, decades ago, much more out of the medical model, where, in Western medicine, the physician is taught that they're in charge. It's a hindrance. And we're convinced that some of the distrust many people have in their therapist and their physician is rooted in the extent to which people have been told simply to trust the authority figure in the room. Perhaps people have been too trusting, and now there's a kind of backlash. So the healthy way forward, it seems to us, is to make the authority be co-defined by patient and therapist.

And that authority isn't simply co-defined, but also collaborative. Richard's first supervisor probably spent 90 percent of the supervision time trying to convince him that he needed to make interpretations and statements rather than simply ask questions, and to be more definitive in what he said. Rather than "Could it be . . ."or "Isn't it possible . . .," the supervisor wanted Richard to just come out and say, "This is what you're experiencing." The interpretation would be much more direct. But in our decades of experience, as we've accumulated more and more knowledge about what may be going on with patients, fortunately, we've come to appreciate a more collaborative understanding of what needs to happen. You may see it this way, but your therapist sees it another way. So before you proceed, you have to deal with that issue between the two of you. And there needs to be room for conflict. If there isn't some degree of conflict—however measured and contained—there may not be any opportunity for change.

For whatever reason, we tend to encounter a lot of patients who want to be told what to do. And we can work with that. If somebody wants us to tell them what to do, we don't mind starting there. That's where they are. We don't simply tell them, "Well, you have to change that," unless we think they need an antagonistic relationship to make progress. Generally, we take whatever the person is doing and go with them, rather than against them. But at the same time, we don't want to get into the situation of creating an unhealthy dependence.

There's a difference between being *dependable*—showing up on time, being consistent, being available—and encouraging a *dependency* of implying, "You need to check with me about everything that you're doing," or that we have some greater wisdom. It's more cooperative, more collaborative.

---

One of the things that changes behavior in general is how conflicts between the patient and the therapist are handled. There needs to be the repair of any relationship so that it can go forward. That's both dealing with issues of conflict in a very different way than what patients have ordinarily experienced because it's real, not just transference, and also making sure they have the experience of empowerment. Making real change in your life can be very empowering because *you* have to do it. Your therapist, or anyone else, cannot do it for you. It's a kind of taking charge that you might never have experienced before, and it can be life changing.

So how do we deal with conflict? Fortunately, we have a great deal of research on how people manage conflicts. It's been well researched. How you learn to deal with conflicts in your childhood becomes part of your personality, which informs how you're going to try to deal with conflicts in adulthood. People will generally go with one primary method: Either they'll withdraw, or they'll push back. Some people argue, and escalate as they argue, as a way of trying to impose their will on the other. Stonewalling, withdrawal, arguing, and pleasing are all ways people learn to deal with conflict. And often those are quite observable in the conflict that will come up in their therapy. So therapy is a good place to work on it.

It's no small thing to understand the power dynamic in the therapeutic relationship, as much for what it says about you as for what it says about the nature of the relationship you cultivate with your therapist. Be alerted to any tendency you may have to want to be told what to do, or any determination not to be told what to do, as well as to a therapist's desire to tell you what to do. All those dynamics will inform whether you're truly able to get the help you need.

# CHAPTER 15

# What if My Therapist Won't Focus on My Immediate Need?

One of the reasons people can be skeptical of therapy is that, when they feel a pressing need to address a specific problem, they may encounter a therapist who wants to talk about bigger, deeper issues. After all, when we go to a physician because we have knee pain, we want the doctor to examine our sore knee. If they start looking at our stomach instead, we're inclined to be suspicious.

But what if the reason our knee is sore is that it's carrying too much weight around? What if the problem with that knee really is rooted somewhere else? We can get a cortisone shot in the knee, but that's just a temporary fix. The pain might subside, but it will return.

Therapy can be like that, too. Let's say you're struggling with anxiety. If, for example, somebody comes to the office and they're having panic attacks, we're not going to get to their deeper issues until the panic abates. So initially, we need to work with the person to help develop the coping skills to be able to tolerate anxiety, because it's not only reducing the panic, but also building in some of the resources that they will need for longer term work— *healing* their anxiety.

If you're at the point of feeling panic, then medication for panic is very useful, because it's so difficult to live when your body and mind are panicking. Sometimes approaches that appear to have some initial short-term effectiveness actually delay the process and make it longer, because you can, in essence, limp along just enough to get by, but not enough to really have the impetus to create the new conditions necessary for healing to occur. We see patients with a lifelong pattern of attempting short-term solutions; that's become the pattern of their life. That may be a good reason for the therapist to not join them. Sometimes a quick fix makes no sense. It might be quite the opposite.

If you come to us with a fear of flying, and you need to get on a plane next week, and you need our help to do that, we can help with that. Therapists want to help however we can. But we might say, "When we finish this up, there's more work to do. I know you have to get on the plane, but there are going to be other issues that come up as we talk about this that will be important to return to." To return to the sore knee analogy, it's the equivalent of giving you the cortisone shot right away, but in the long run, you're still going to need to think about weight loss. That fear of flying may be the symptom of something larger, and until we know what that something larger is, you'll keep encountering piecemeal problems and needing piecemeal solutions.

We know that there are immediate needs to be met, but still, we want to turn the question around. When you ask only to address an immediate need, we want to ask, "Why do you settle for so little? Why is that all you're asking for? If you could be changing your experience, entering into life in a different way, why wouldn't you want that? Why would you only pick at the corners, rather than feasting on the whole meal?"

And we might ask a follow-up question, "How typical is that for you to settle for so little? Do you do that in other settings? Is this part of how you approach life?" These are the sorts of questions a good therapist might ask. We want to get at the root of what's keeping you from flourishing. We understand that you're busy; we all are now. But what if we could help you into something more?

If you go to therapy in search of a solution to an immediate need, and a therapist is able to help you with it, you could consider that a gateway to a larger conversation. That's often how it goes in therapy. Most of our patients come to us in search of a specific answer to a specific problem. It could be as simple as a fear of flying, or a fear of giving a big speech, or something else that feels momentous. Others come to us in times of transition; they want to figure out how to handle a promotion, or a lack of promotion, or retirement, or the death of a family member. A few will come to us with a vague sense that they're stuck, that life isn't moving forward in some important way, and they want to understand why. It's usually a crisis of some sort that brings people to us. Not very many people enter therapy just come to have open-ended conversations about life.

If a therapist can help you address a particular need, that may prompt you to consider becoming more ambitious in your therapy. We've seen how much good therapy can do. Good therapy really can help you flourish. It can help you understand things you didn't understand about yourself before. It can help you understand your problematic responses to particular situations, or your repeated patterns that may frustrate you and others. It may help you get unstuck in contexts in which you couldn't even see how stuck you were.

When you get to the point where therapy has met that immediate need, we might be inclined to say, "Since you made so much progress here, congratulations! Now we can go further. What's your rush? We're just getting started. There are all kinds of different ways we may be able to help." That can trigger suspicion in some people, a sense that we're just looking for more work and more money. Maybe some therapists have done that in some cases, but right now, as we've mentioned elsewhere, therapists are all booked up. Most of us really don't need the work. So if we're asking you to stay at it, we probably have better reasons than you might suspect.

So, use the occasion of the immediate need you're facing to see whether you've got a therapist who can be trusted to help you. And then, if you do, keep exploring. If you're ambitious enough to try, you may be able to find ways of flourishing that you can't yet even imagine.

# CHAPTER 16

# How Can I Tell If I'm Making Progress?

As therapy progresses, feelings will surface. You might start feeling better right away, but you might start feeling worse. That might seem like a terrible red flag: You went to therapy so you could start feeling better, and now you feel awful instead?

If that happens, stick with it. That awful feeling might mean you're actually making progress.

Sometimes with a physical problem you feel worse before you feel better—if you're going through chemotherapy, for example. But more often, if you take your medicine or you otherwise follow a physician's recommendations, you'll start feeling better fairly quickly. That may not be the case in therapy.

Richard once had a patient who had developed, over time, a very hard-shelled, restrictive, super-male identity. He couldn't cry. He couldn't show uncertainty or anxiety. When in doubt, he just plowed straight ahead. And essentially, that's how he maintained order in his life, given a very chaotic, violent family. Richard was working toward getting him to recognize and feel certain feelings. One day the patient got in touch with what it was like, as a young boy, to be on the receiving end of his father's violence, and he broke down in tears. It was very disconcerting to him. He lost all composure; he was completely disheveled. He looked at Richard and said, "Look what you've done to me!"

All Richard said to him was, "Congratulations. You've worked hard for this moment." It was a breakthrough. The patient had suppressed these feelings at a tremendous cost to his body and his relationships most of his adult life.

Of course, there can be happier breakthroughs, too. There can be a powerfully good feeling that comes with a moment of understanding and clarity. We've said that therapy is co-created, that while a therapist can guide and help, ultimately a patient has to own the process and make a positive change. Realizing that you can do that can be a wonderful feeling.

For us, the point of therapy isn't to make you feel good or feel bad. In a sense, there is no such thing as a bad feeling. Feelings that are painful help us identify danger and help us survive. If patients start feeling better, we're delighted. We'll take it. But then the follow-up question has to be, "What are you going to do with the feeling?" It's only going to have value if it leads to something else. Feeling better is not a stopping point or even the goal. The goal of therapy is to live better.

Your therapist might have a different idea of progress than you. Because they're more familiar with the process, they know that as people start to make changes, often what they might think of as progress, such as reduced depression or anxiety, doesn't occur. In fact, it often goes the other direction, as it did with Richard's male patient.

Anxiety increases, depression increases, particularly at the beginning. If a person erects all sorts of walls to manage their life with their parents or with their culture, for example, and they start to tear down those so-called *emotionally protective walls*, and they start to open up, they will start to identify what they're feeling underneath. That awareness may well feel more frightened, like when somebody is addicted to alcohol and they stop using alcohol, they feel worse. Alcohol was a source of comfort. And it may well feel like they're regressing instead of progressing. It's very important to talk to your therapist about this and listen to what the therapist will say on the basis of experience. Because your feelings may not be telling you the truth about what's happening.

Sometimes it's difficult to know exactly when progress is being made because it can be a felt experience before it surfaces as a concrete change. When we were in training, we were told that behavior is the last thing to change in therapy, that thoughts and feelings would change first. That's often the case. And surprisingly, sometimes behavioral change indicates that therapy is stalled. That may indicate a flight from changed behavior to avoid dealing with deeper, more troubling issues. It serves a defensive purpose.

Sometimes progress is disconnected from behavior, but comes subtly, with a different perspective. You might experience a different feeling, or an expanded awareness. Sometimes a patient can be aware of it, and sometimes it takes the therapist to point it out. That's one of the reasons that a collaborative approach is so important: The therapist who stays close to the patient's experience is much better able to underscore and build on the changes that are occurring. Inside awareness about what's happening frequently comes after—not before—change occurs. You figure out why you're doing something after you stop or start doing it.

We think it's important for therapists to check with patients about how they see therapy, and how they see the relationship with their therapist. At the end of a particularly difficult session when the person is having trouble organizing themselves to leave, we might ask them, "What's the biggest takeaway from the session today?" That triggers the cognitive process to evaluate the experience, to solidify change, to think about change, and then to behaviorally implement it. We might ask for some evaluation—not of us or of the therapy, necessarily, but of the relationship. "How are we doing? How are we working together? What's your sense of it? Are we connecting? Are we going where you thought where we would be going?"

Bear in mind that it's not always for the best if we're going exactly where you thought we would or should be going. Going where you wanted to go could be a bad thing, or it could be a good thing. If we're simply following expectations, we need ask whether there are different avenues closed off that they need to open up. There needs to be some positive connection, some positive transference to move forward. But there should probably be at least some surprises in therapy, or else it may not be doing what it could.

Your therapist needs to be aware of *pacing* and the *rate of change*. A patient may want a radical shift, to make a big change and just kind of jump into something. They may need to be slowed down a bit to help regulate the change, because too much too soon, can be as destructive as not enough change. So much depends on the relationship, and if the therapist is inviting responses about what's going right and what's going wrong, or what might seem like too little and what might seem like too much, for example, then all those responses can help guide and shape the necessary change. Is change occurring at the rate or as broadly as is necessary, and as both the patient and therapist think is best?

It turns out that making progress in therapy isn't as simple as it sounds. It can be a winding road, and sometimes even feel like a series of setbacks. But hang in there. If it feels hard, if it feels challenging, if it feels surprising, that just might mean that something important is happening.

## CHAPTER 17

# What If Therapy Makes My Life Harder Instead of Easier?

"I don't want to talk about it."

A lot of us feel that way a lot of the time. Something is bothering us, but we have to stay at work, or we have to get the groceries, or we have to do any one of a hundred things. So we don't unpack that nagging thought, that vaguely unsettled feeling. We just leave it, or we ignore it, or maybe we cope with it by eating or drinking or sleeping.

Another way of saying that is that we often choose chronic pain over acute pain. It's the devil we know rather than the devil we don't. What if therapy unleashes the devil we don't know, and it's too big and too difficult to face?

There are different kinds of *difficult*, of course. Therapy can point out some of the seriousness entailed in life's choices. It can make clear that there are real consequences for choosing one path over another, engaging in this behavior and not in that one. And there is certainly an element of suffering that accompanies awareness. That doesn't mean that one engages in therapy in a masochistic way, or to create unnecessary pain. But therapy is supposed to do is help you face the realities of life.

Therapy does move people in the direction of pain, sometimes. That sounds a little strange. But that's a lot of what therapy is about, which is getting people to accept some painful things that have happened. We have parents that have let us down, friends that have disappointed us, people that have abandoned us. A lot of therapy is about acceptance of the pain. And it helps people deal not just with the pain, but also with what they've done to try to avoid pain, which is often making their life even more difficult. They've self-medicated with alcohol, for example, with all the predictable problems that alcohol can bring.

And therapy can uncover trauma, which can be awful to face. We know that trauma leaves a very deep imprint on our brains, bodies, and minds; the pain keeps us from turning toward love and presence and what light is available. Going back inside to try to avoid pain is usually where even more problems occur. Grieving painful experiences is an important part of healing, and often people are handicapped in grieving in part because they have been told in so many ways not to grieve, to get over it, to move on.

Therapy, then, is really about learning to be with your pain, not building a defense around it, not closing up your heart because of it, not taking on too much responsibility, or avoiding any responsibility. We have so many ways of distracting ourselves, everything from our cell phones to our ideologies, to getting busy with work and adding to our treasure chest. These avoidances take us away from our own inner self. That's what we tend to do with trauma—we disconnect from the self to manage whatever physical or emotional pain is happening. So our goal in therapy is to stop running from the pain, to face it, to understand where it's coming from and what it's doing to us so that we can begin to bend our lives in a different direction, a more loving direction, with greater self-acceptance.

It's important to realize that therapy isn't what's causing the pain. It only reveals the source of the pain. The source isn't always easy to uncover on our own. Sometimes the pain happens so early in life that we don't know its source. If it happens at age two, or three, or four, it's still imprinted in our bodies, in our brains. We adapt as children to handle stress. We accommodate it to get by, and then that adaptation becomes a way of life. And that's where the difficulties arise. Maybe your response is to become too responsible, or not responsible enough. Maybe you've become too withdrawn, or too outgoing. All those adaptations can make life worse, even though they might seem to protect you from the more acute pain you'd rather not face.

But maybe you're not really feeling what you'd call pain right now. We rarely have patients who come and simply say, "I'm in pain." Instead they'll say, "I'm stuck," or "This thing just happened to me." Maybe they just found out their spouse is having an affair. Obviously, that's painful. They're talking about it in a protective way by talking about what's happening outside of themselves. And often in those early sessions what's usually presented are the ways in which someone has tried to manage the pain—the defensive structure. It takes time to unpack that, to see what they're protecting. They present with the exterior, the false self, which is so used to accommodating and adapting; that protects the much more vulnerable, real self. They don't know how to talk about it from the inside. They're talking about the external event, as if that were the pain. No, the pain is on the inside. It's the damage that was done. In therapy, we can work through the things that have caused us pain to discover its source.

That still might sound like something you don't really want to face. Like it or not, you might have a fear of taking action. Maybe facing the pain you're feeling will need to lead to action. Maybe you need a divorce, or to find a new job, or to change your circumstances in some other way. That's a common point for people to come into therapy. When they need to make a decision that could change their life and they don't know what's happens next or who they'll be on the other side.

In situations like these—feeling stuck or feeling the momentousness of getting out of being stuck—people are often fear their emotions when they decide to seek therapy. They're afraid of feeling too deeply. If they cry they'll never be able to stop. If they begin to express anger they'll lose control completely. They might feel like their loneliness or depression could kill them. So often the fear is not about thinking, but about the emotional sense of coming apart at the seams. That needs to be carefully managed by a skilled therapist. Because the simple fact is that there may very well need to be a kind of coming apart, a kind of losing control, in order to understand what's really happening in your life. It's a therapist's job not simply to get you to open up, but to guide you through that process in a way that you can also recover and heal.

That's one of the reasons therapists aren't necessarily wise to establish the course of treatment in the first couple of sessions. Your problem with alcohol or codependency, or anything else might, be the thing you want to change, but that behavior pattern might be rooted in a deeper source. So stay with it, and together with your therapist you can treat not just the symptoms, but the very root of a problem that feels like it might never go away.

## CHAPTER 18

# What If Therapy Makes Me Feel Like a Terrible Person?

A lot of us feel guilt or shame at some point in our lives. That's one of those lurking senses within us. And because therapists are experts in mental health, they are a kind of authority figure. We've all had authority figures in our lives—parents, teachers, priests, and even doctors. They provide guidance, and sometimes they to pass judgment on a test, or a confession, or some bad behavior. So what if you decide to see a therapist and you just end up feeling judged—whether from the therapist or from yourself? What if you just start feeling like a terrible person? Or, if you already think you might be a terrible person, what if you go into therapy and the therapist removes all doubt?

If you're getting good therapy, you're going to learn new things about yourself. You're going to see with greater clarity things that you might have just wondered about or suspected. And you may not like everything you learn about yourself, just like when you go to the doctor's office, or to church, or to a family member's house. An important part of a diagnosis is understanding why you are where you are and how you got here. And just as it's difficult to forgive someone else before you know what they've done, it may be difficult to forgive yourself—until you understand what's really going on.

We need to make a distinction between shame and guilt. *Guilt* is feeling bad for something you've *done*. You violated your own code. You've done something that doesn't sit right. Guilt is something that we can do something about. And by the way, if you never feel guilt, that's a huge problem. That's associated with sociopathic behavior. So if someone tells you that guilt is something to simply be gotten past, they may not be on the right track. As a society and as individuals, we need a sense of guilt when people do wrong. "Don't worry, be happy" is not a wise response to bad behavior, either for yourself, or for those you love, or for the world you live in.

*Shame*, on the other hand, is much more difficult to face. It goes much deeper. It is about your value as a person. It's about who you are, not simply a thing you've done. Shame lives in the darkness, and it eats away at us. And it's closely tied to fear, because so often in human history we have used shame to mark people as unacceptable or to be excluded. Societies once put disgraced people on display in the center of town, and townspeople would go by and throw things at them. Shame has been used to expel people from communities, and when we feel shame we often feel unworthy to be loved or accepted. It's the sinking feeling that, when people find out the truth about us, they will find us so unworthy that they'll send us away. It goes to the very heart of our identity and our place in the world.

So what can you expect if guilt or shame comes up in therapy?

We'll address the various benefits of group therapy in another chapter, but for now we'll say that one of its benefits is to help people deal with shame. In one-on-one therapy, they might expect a therapist to be on their side, or at least to be empathetic. But what happens when it's time to face a larger group? Sometimes if a patient is feeling shame, we might have them face the group. We might have them stand because, otherwise, they'll want to shrink and crumble. And we'll often have them look directly at the other group members. We'll tell them to trust their eyes rather than their feelings. Because if they look, they'll see that others aren't rejecting them, even though their feelings might be saying something very different. That's part of why Alcoholics

Anonymous and other twelve-step groups have been so effective. They help people get over their shame—their fear of what will happen if others see them for who they are.

---

Kirk had one particularly powerful group experience regarding guilt and shame. A man in his group had, for some time, gotten the group very angry at his ex-wife and at his daughter. He would talk about going to see them and the door being slammed in his face. But then, after doing this for several sessions, he worked up the courage to say that he had sexually abused his daughter. Now the others understood why the ex-wife slammed the door in his face. But what was so powerful was that they could see what he'd been doing, and they didn't reject him for it. They saw how he'd been working up to finally admitting what he'd done. They didn't condone sexually abusing his daughter, but they saw what he was struggling with in talking to them. They had compassion for him in his finding the courage to admit it his shame.

That was the beginning of a healing experience for him, but importantly, the healing wasn't simply soothing his feelings. Over time, over the next several years, he contacted his daughter. He wrote to her. He patiently waited her out. He presented many options. Would she be willing to meet with him and his therapist? Would it be okay if her therapist came and met with them? Could they have a telephone call? He did not give up until finally she was able to face him.

When it came time to talk about the possibility of forgiveness, he took three important steps. First, he told her very specifically what he had done, without offering excuses. He didn't try to get her to understand what drove him. He said quite clearly, "I did this, it was wrong, and I have great sorrow for my actions." He didn't say things like, "I can never forgive myself for that," which might sound like a good thing to say, but really it's a way to garner sympathy. By the time the patient got to that point, he knew saying something like that would be manipulative. Second, he asked straight out, "Will you forgive me?" He was prepared for her to say no, which she did. Then he said, "Will you think about it? And if you ever change your mind, will you let me know?" And then third, when she did say she was willing to forgive him—and she had certain things that she wanted to say with that—he said, "Is there anything I can do to make it right?"

Along the way, his therapist and his group helped him face the consequences of his actions and didn't let him take any easy ways out. They led him through a terrible feeling to something far better than mere soothing or affirmation; they helped bring about reconciliation.

Whether you're carrying guilt, or shame, or some potent mixture of the two, don't avoid therapy just to avoid feeling worse. Because something far better may be waiting for you.

CHAPTER 19

# How Can I Tell If My Therapist is Crossing a Line?

Psychotherapy is intimate, private, and deeply personal. Doing it well requires vulnerability—sometimes from the therapist as well as the patient. It's a relationship in which unknown or unexpressed desires, conflicts, questions, and dreams may be explored. For this unveiling process to occur, the therapist must reveal some humanity, kindness, and compassion, no matter what technique they're using. Patients can feel a broad range of intense emotions, including anger, fear, despair, and love.

For many years, therapists were trained to be stoic with their patients, to keep rigid boundaries, and to avoid showing any emotion. There was plenty of psychoanalytic theory behind that approach, but it was also safer, too. Everyone knew the rules. And while the field is changing concerning the emotional relationship of therapist to patient, there are still boundaries that must be respected—on both sides.

In the emotional intensity of a therapy session, if the therapist can engage and not be frightened off by the emotion, the therapy can progress as misunderstandings are addressed, ruptures repaired, and emotions integrated. A good therapist is a trusted, calm ally who can be present for patient's self-scrutiny and questioning.

Or at least that's how it's supposed to go.

The problem is that therapists are as human as anyone else. Sometimes they're lonely, or depressed, and they may look for an inappropriate relationship as a way to address it. Some of them develop an inflated sense of their own attractiveness and charisma. Some of them might believe that they're owed something for all the emotional work they're doing. Maybe they feel deeply loved by a patient in ways that simply aren't true. They may well be loved, but for what they represent rather than who they are; it's what Sigmund Freud called, and we still call, *transference*.

There are many reasons for such boundary violations, and we cannot stress this enough: *None of them are good.* Therapists violate their moral responsibility by taking advantage of a patient's vulnerability to meet their own needs.

For whatever reason, sometimes therapists simply do bad things, and because patients have made themselves vulnerable, the therapist might know all too well just how to take advantage of them.

Moves toward seduction can be subtle and unfold slowly:

1. Your therapist might routinely extend session times.
2. They might suggest a change in appointment time to the final hour of the day without giving a good explanation.
3. They might comment on your looks—on how attractive you are, or how particularly good you look today.
4. They might compliment you in other ways that don't really have anything to do with therapy. They might spontaneously talk about how special you are, or how no one seems to appreciate you, or how you really understand them or their work better than anyone else does.
5. They might overstep boundaries by beginning to talk about their own problems in ways that have nothing to do with your therapy, thereby making themselves seems needy and vulnerable in a way that might invite you into their personal lives inappropriately.

6. They might be too solicitous. For example, they might call you when you haven't asked to be called or otherwise reach out to you in unrequested ways.
7. They might touch you after a session—maybe a hand on the shoulder, or a rub on the back. Or they might really make things confusing by asking you whether you feel like you need a hug.

If you experience any of these, or anything else that seems even a little inappropriate, the first thing you need to do is trust yourself. You have every right to ask questions about your patient-therapist interactions. Don't simply go along with any therapist who doesn't welcome that. You shouldn't keep your concerns to yourself.

---

Often, simply asking questions will be enough to stop the behavior. It can clear up misunderstandings, and most of all, it can warn the seductive therapist that you suspect something. That warning is by itself is sometimes enough to get things back on a better footing.

If, however, the therapist becomes defensive, or accusatory, or attempts to shame or humiliate you, then it is *time to leave*, plain and simple.

Or the question may prompt a torrent of emotions in response, as the therapist unloads about everything they've been going through, or how bad they feel. Simply put, if you are in the position of taking care of your therapist, that signals the end of that therapy experience. That's not the relationship you signed up for or should expect.

Sometimes love, or some form of it, may be expressed in therapy. In a relationship of vulnerability, where one person can be of such great help to another, it wouldn't be surprising for that to emerge. But it can be confusing, frightening, and fraught with potential risk for both patient and therapist. So even as you make yourself as vulnerable as you need to be to make progress in your therapy, stay alert, and know what to look for. Therapy may not always feel safe, but you should always be able to feel safe with your therapist.

## CHAPTER 20

# How Do I Know If I'm Getting Bad Therapy?

We've all heard horror stories about bad therapy. Some of us have even lived them. It can be a dawning realization or a sudden insight: *This is not helpful.* How do you know whether to trust that feeling?

We begin by asking that question because it's important to realize that discomfort isn't necessarily a bad thing. There's a difference between the discomfort that can come from making progress in therapy and discomfort that comes from bad therapy. As we said before, sometimes feeling awful is in fact a sign that you're making a breakthrough; sometimes your therapist is doing something that needs to be done. But there are plenty of bad reasons to be uncomfortable in therapy, too.

Good therapy begins with a therapist's appropriate presentation of themselves. They need to make it clear that they take this relationship seriously as a *professional* relationship. They should be dressed appropriately. They should be on time for your appointment. They shouldn't be double-booking you or forgetting appointments. They shouldn't cancel on you at the last minute. If they're going to be unavailable because they're on vacation, they should let you know and arrange for coverage.

A therapist's behavior should be appropriate and attentive and reflect the fact that you're paying for their time and attention. They shouldn't be munching on a snack. They shouldn't interrupt you to answer a phone call or a text, or to check a message. They should be able to track your conversation, to remember names and other key information. And they should never, ever fall asleep on you.

Good boundaries are important in therapy. Your therapist shouldn't have a chummy nickname for you or use profanity in a way that's meant to impress you or make the conversation seem casual. They might refer to another patient's situation, but only in a way that could be helpful for you, and not in any way that compromises a confidence. You have every right to expect that your therapist will keep confidences, and you should pay attention for any sign that that isn't happening.

There's a very particular form of intimacy that develops in therapy, but you should always be alert to whether it's the right *kind* of intimacy, because there are many forms of intimacy that can range from uncomfortable to clear and obvious breaches of ethics and even outright harassment.

Pay attention to excesses such as tight-fitting clothing. If you're describing a problem with sex, it is important that they not ask for more detail than they need. Similarly, pay attention if they draw attention to their attractiveness, or fish for compliments, or make excessive remarks on your attractiveness, or on what you're wearing and how it flatters you. They may talk about their own sex lives in a way that feels intrusive. The list could go on and on.

It is best if physical contact, such as a hug, occur in group therapy rather than individual therapy. This way others can observe and comment if it looks inappropriate. In any case, the therapist should always ask permission for any touch—and it would be wise for them to ask if you feel free to say no. Unwanted touching or having with your therapist is not part of the healing process.

But intimacy doesn't have to be sexual to be inappropriate, either. That hug you're being offered should not be a false or forced closeness that you may not feel comfortable with yet—or ever. Your therapist should have a sense of that.

Of course, things can go wrong in a very different direction, too. Maybe the therapist isn't trying to connect with you inappropriately when the therapist isn't really trying to connect with you at all! Bad therapy can be aloof, distant, or even condescending.

---

Therapy is best if it is a form of guidance that never becomes manipulative. It is best if you have the sense that your therapist is in charge, knows what they're doing, and knows useful pathways to try. But it is also best when you have the sense that you and your therapist are on the same page, that you desire the same ultimate outcome of the process.

Your therapist may experience vulnerability in therapy—or, alternatively, not be vulnerable enough. But these opposite feelings can present similarly as a kind of defensive superiority. They might use language meant to show you just how much learning they've acquired. They might convey the sense that the way they see things is the only way those things should be seen. It is important that they do not become dismissive when you object to something they're saying or become defensive and fight back. It may be important for them to argue with you, but not to the point of becoming argumentative. Similarly, it is bad practice for them to turn the argument back on you by getting personal in ways that improperly expose a vulnerability in you.

Your therapist ideally will be flexible and not become rigid with you in ways that do not help and do not meet you in your particular context. It is also best that they are not too oriented toward feelings in a moment when you're trying to understand something intellectually—or vice versa. It is also problematic if they become too clinical at a vulnerable moment. It is important that they not spiritualize something for which you need intellectual understanding or are dismissive if you are a person of faith who feels your most deeply held values being disregarded.

What do all these red flags have in common? They all represent ways that therapists can put themselves first—their needs, their anxieties, their desires. They're all ways of not hearing what you need or offering what you need. They're all circumstances that can breed frustration and even a sense of helplessness.

If you're getting this feeling from your therapy, we have these questions: What's stopping you from leaving? Are you afraid of breaking the relationship? If so, why? Do you just feel too overwhelmed to find someone else?

Therapy is an involved relationship and ending it can almost feel like breaking up. We should know; we have broken up with, and been broken up with, by many patients and several other therapists. But we all know that breakups sometimes simply need to happen, as difficult as they may be.

When it's time to end a bad therapeutic relationship, tell the truth. You don't have to spell out every last detail—but be honest. You might say, "Thank you for what you have provided me, but I'm really looking for a different kind of experience, the kind of experience that I don't believe you're able to provide." You have the right to do that—and the responsibility, both to the therapist and ultimately to yourself.

## CHAPTER 21

# What are the Hallmarks of Good Therapy?

Therapy is a commitment. It's not really possible to do a lot of comparison shopping in therapy; we have to choose someone and, absent some obvious red flags, we need to stick with that person for a while in order to find out whether they're a good fit. And it's that fit that really matters because good therapy is a relationship. But as you explore that relationship, what should you look for? What traits might a therapist display that help you see promise for a good working relationship?

We're going to try to make this easier for you by coming up with a list. To make it even easier, we'll provide a list of traits that all begin with the letter "C."

**Competency.** We mention this one first because it's so important. Yes, it speaks to training, which is crucial. You want a therapist who has gotten the right kind of degree, the right kind of certification. But those only go so far. Your therapist doesn't have to have an Ivy League degree in order to be well trained, but the basics do have to be there—some sort of master's degree at a minimum, ranging up to a doctorate. And of course they need to be certified, too, which means they have completed a baseline number of hours doing supervised work, and in some cases they might need to complete some coursework occasionally in order to maintain certification.

But the degree and the certification constitute only a very basic threshold. They have to be there, but you should want more, too. We have always been helped, when receiving therapy, by therapists who've clearly kept up on their reading with the latest developments in the field. Human understanding of the mind and of the mind-body connection, keeps evolving, and you don't want a therapist who is content to stand still and rest on whatever they learned in graduate school. You want a physician whose learning is up to date; you'll want that in a therapist, too.

**Curiosity.** This one flows naturally from the first characteristic. You want a therapist who is curious—not just about the latest developments in the field, but about you. You'll want them to ask a lot of questions about you. No two therapeutic relationships are exactly alike, because no two patients are exactly alike. If the therapist's mind is on the move, they will be looking for ways to tie what they've learned to your unique circumstances. That curiosity allows the relationship to grow and evolve.

It can be easy—too easy—for a therapist to fall into certain ruts, ones that may have served them well more than once but now threaten their ability to really help you. Curiosity includes wondering whether a particular approach is working. It includes wondering whether it's wise to try something different as well as wondering, *Why this symptom now? What is it expressing? What is it hiding?* Maybe asking you such questions sometimes. And don't be afraid to ask those questions yourself. Good therapy isn't a passive process.

One more thing about curiosity: *It is different than being judgmental.* The TV show *Ted Lasso* misattributed this quote, "Be curious, not judgmental," to Walt Whitman, but the idea still stands. Carl Jung said, "Thinking is difficult. That is why most people judge." Your therapist's first job is to be curious, but not judgmental. It's very difficult to make permanent change from a posture of defensiveness or a simple assertion of willpower. Therapist and patient alike do best to understand *why* something is happening.

**Creativity.** This is a big one. You want a therapist who has different tools they might be able to use to help you, but also the creativity to know which tools to try, and when. And you can see how all of these are interrelated. It's hard for a therapist to be creative if they don't have the tools (competency) and they're not constantly thinking about ways they could use them to help you (curiosity). There are a range of tools available for therapists to learn about and use, methods such as hypnosis, body work, or visualization. Group therapy can also be helpful. And patients might be in more than one of these therapies at once.

A good therapist won't go in with a roadmap; they'll try different things, always alert to what might be evolving in their relationship with the patient. And not every therapist is trained in every possible technique. For example, Kirk is trained in hypnosis, but Richard isn't. We each lead group therapy, but you'd have a different experience in our different groups. No one therapist has to know every conceivable approach, but a good therapist has a range of training to draw upon and develops a sense of what different techniques to try at which point in the relational work.

**Character.** Here's where we begin to move from the way a therapist thinks to certain innate characteristics best to look for in someone you're going to trust. The first of these is what we'll call *character*. To us, character in a therapist comes down to two traits—integrity and self-discipline.

Integrity in therapy is an integration of the whole person—thoughts, feelings, and behavior. A therapist has integrity when they can hold all these things together in themselves, to understand the role they all play and how they relate to one another. They understand their own impulses and the origins of those impulses. We might also call it self-awareness. This is one of the goals of good therapy—to raise self-awareness—and as usual, you want a therapist who practices what they preach.

You also want a therapist with self-discipline. A therapist may feel like they want to say or do something just to change for the sake of change, not really having anything specific in mind apart from meeting their own needs. They may be bored and want to stir something up. Or a therapist might have a very attractive patient who dresses seductively, but it's not commented on, and in fact the therapist rather enjoys it, and it's communicated indirectly, through eyesight that lingers a little too long, for example. You want a therapist who disciplines their approach, their ethics, their desires—even their billing. Often people come to therapy asking for help with self-discipline. Therapy will go best when the therapist already understands and uses it.

**Courage**. This one may be surprising. But if therapists encourage patients to be courageous, they do best to be courageous, too. A patient will have to show courage in order to overcome fear or anxiety. But therapists often have fear too, especially the fear of failure, or the fear that patients will see a weakness or shortcoming. A good therapist does best having the courage to admit failures or shortcomings. We have had patients who've disagreed with us—and been right. We're always grateful to learn about ways to do something better, but that hasn't necessarily come easily. Admitting you're wrong takes courage, and it's important for a therapist, as well as a patient, to display that courage.

Courage is not the same as willpower. Courage brings you to the point that you risk stepping into something with an unknown outcome. It's different, it's new, it's frightening, it has a very unfinished quality to it. It means stepping into something that you've been afraid to try, but in the context of this relationship, a therapist will want you to become more courageous. They need to be courageous, too—to be able to move into a new way of thinking, one they might even learn from you.

**Compassion.** This one is essential for healing. And it's not sympathy; it's more like a healthy empathy. It requires vulnerability and humility, on the part of the therapist as well as the patient. Compassion has to do with a genuine *we-ness. We* experience this or that hard thing. It's painful at times, it's scary at times, but it's part of life. And you can feel it when it's in the room. A therapist often needs to help a patient find self-compassion, and in order to do so, therapists show genuine compassion themselves.

This can create a deep emotional connection, and that has to be guarded carefully. In fact, therapists used to be warned against showing emotion; that was labeled as *countertransference*, and it was considered unprofessional. But we have come to believe in the importance of genuine compassion. Sometimes we're moved to tears by what our patients are going through. There's nothing wrong with that, as long as healthy boundaries are maintained. In fact, it can be a vital part of helping patients to give themselves the compassion they need.

**Caring.** This last one on the list is in some ways the most important one—the capstone of the list. It's essential. As a patient, it is important to feel valued by your therapist. So often people come to therapy because past relationships have been damaging, and in most cases, the earlier that damage occurred the more significant the problems. And while unconsciously you may be looking for a kind of idealized parent in a therapist, we believe it's important to encounter a sense of genuine care.

Only recently have people in our field begun to acknowledge that therapists, particularly therapists who work on a long-term basis, can love their patients. It's not a romantic love, but it's a deep affection. That becomes important not only to form a supportive foundation for the relationship, but it also allows the therapist to, for example, confront certain resistances or certain behaviors, ways of thinking, reactions, from a place where the patient knows that there is legitimate and real concern. The tone would not be bossy or bullying; it would come from a place of genuine affection.

Healing takes place in the context of healthy, caring relationship. So it's okay for your therapist to care about you. In fact, we think that's a very good thing. They must observe good boundaries; that's part of having character. And all of the other "C"s matter, too. But finally they all need to come together in the service of caring for you so that you can build a relationship with a therapist that leads to real and lasting healing.

## CHAPTER 22

# If I Run out of Things to Talk About, Am I Done with Therapy?

If you're in therapy, we hope it's going well. We hope you're experiencing some enlightenment about your life, noticing patterns, making healthy changes. But sometimes that sense of success can lead to a lull. There may be a sessions when it just doesn't seem like you have much to talk about. Does that mean you should be done? Is it time to end your therapy?

Well, maybe. But let's talk about that!

It could be a good thing that you don't think you have anything to talk about. It might mean that you're willing to come to the session unprepared, unrehearsed. Having open space in which to talk to a therapist can be good. Coming unprepared might also be beneficial if you've been duty-bound all of your life or have had a natural tendency to please others. Either one of these tendencies might lead you to having an appropriate agenda; but if you're flexible and more spontaneous you may move in a better direction.

A therapist might begin a session in silence so that a patient then has the responsibility of identifying what it is that they want to talk about, and in the process, they might reveal all kinds of personality characteristics about how they handle authority, how they handle open space, or how creative they are. That silence by the therapist might uncover something important to talk about.

On the other hand, it could be problematic if the patient's lack of preparedness reflects a general pattern of not preparing for an encounter in other relationships. We might ask, "How often is this the way you come in for anything? Whether it's therapy or meeting up with a friend, where you haven't thought about what you want to say to them, what you want to get from them, what you want to give to them, that you show up and sort of expect to be taken care of. Is this typical?" After all, therapy isn't cheap, and it's an opportunity to help yourself. Why aren't you doing more work to take advantage of it?

So whether this is a good development or a problematic one is something we may want to talk about with you. Which means having nothing to talk about may in itself be something to talk about—or may lead to something important to explore.

What if this not knowing what to talk about really leaves you wondering whether you're done with therapy?

As we've discussed elsewhere, we're concerned about the desire for therapy designed only to fix one specific problem. It's often not the root problem, which means the quick fix ends up not really fixing anything. So, as we said earlier, it would be wise to talk about whether you're done with therapy, not because we need the work, but instead because you might need help you don't even know what you need.

So if you wonder whether you're done, we're likely to say something like, "Maybe you are. Let's explore it. Let's figure out what has happened so far, what you've gotten, what you haven't gotten. Let's be thoughtful about it."

We would hope you'd be curious about what your therapist thinks and that your relationship with your therapist is trusting enough that you would be able to ask that question—and trust the response.

And if we were your therapist, we probably would explore that a little bit. We might ask, "Are you the kind of person who gets things done very quickly? Because you're doing it a lot quicker than most people. How does that play out in your life, getting things done quickly?" And we would ask you to come up with some examples. Maybe jumping out too soon is costing you something, and it's time to stop and look at that.

By the way, you might wonder how often we decide that a patient is done. The answer is that it doesn't happen very often. Again, we don't think of therapy in terms of a specific problem to be cured, but as an opportunity for growth. And on a personal level, we get invested in our patients, and we would hope our colleagues would, too. There's always more that we can see to do, and if a patient hasn't seen it, we're trying to help them see what we see.

That doesn't mean it never happens. It's important that we make sure that a patient continues to make progress. If they've stalled and aren't constructively using their sessions, and they don't respond to different approaches, talk in circles, or linger on the same issues, they risk undoing of the gains made. If a patient is stuck, continuing to come to therapy can actually be a kind of resistance to taking the next step.

After all, an important goal of therapy is to get you out there, living your life. As much as we want to find every possible way to help you, at some point we know that it's our job to work ourselves out of a job. We want to help; we're invested. But at some point, you might need to move into a new chapter in your life, to take what you've learned in therapy and use it to move in a good direction. Life is short, after all.

So while we're invested and we want to help, we know that there may be a point when the relationship needs to end. It costs money to be in therapy; it takes time and effort.

Before deciding to end therapy, be cautious about assuming that having nothing to talk about means you're done; it could in fact lead to a breakthrough, to a new area of your life that could benefit from exploration. Don't give up too quickly; talk it through with your therapist. But if you really are done, you should know that there's a great deal of value in ending well. It is best that the process not be ended abruptly.

That's the subject of the final section of this book: How do you know when to get out, and how do you do so in a way that you can move forward and allows you to flourish in the next stage of your life? How do you make sure you take what you need when you leave?

CHAPTER 23

# When Should I End Therapy?

Even though we believe in the power of good therapy and a longstanding relationship with a therapist who can help you make sense of yourself and how you interact with those around you, we know that sooner or later every patient-therapist relationship needs to end. That is, after all, the point of therapy—to get to the point where it's no longer needed. So how do you know when that time has come?

We've both been in therapy with a number of different therapists, and we've both made the decision to end therapy in different contexts.

One reason to end therapy is simply the sense that you're no longer getting what you need. While we're both suspicious of going to therapy for a quick fix for one particular problem, we know that patients need what they need, and that it's not their job simply to remain in therapy endlessly while the therapist isn't progressing. You might develop the sense that your therapist may be especially helpful in one area but not in another. That's not uncommon, and it's something to keep an eye out for.

The first therapist Richard saw really helped him deal with issues related to his father, but when it came time to talk about his mother, the therapist didn't seem to have any insights that helped. It wasn't until relatively recently, in the last couple of years, that Richard found a therapist who he thought really could help with issues related to his mother. Just because a therapist's approach seems especially helpful in one area of your life doesn't mean that that person can help in every area.

When you begin to feel like the therapeutic relationship is stagnating, you might wonder, *Is it the therapist? Is it me? Or is this how therapy goes?* At that point, it is best to speak frankly with your therapist about what you're experiencing. It's not always easy to tell. Sometimes when the patient feels that way, the relationship is reaching a plateau. Or, it may be on the precipice of a breakthrough; or sometimes it's really coming to an end.

Plateaus in therapy can feel like you're rehashing the same issues. But an effective therapist will work to figure out a way through by trying different strategies to get things moving again. A true plateau can lead to growth. There's a sense of agitation, a feeling that there's something more; *can't quite get it, I don't know what it is.* There's something that's not quite in awareness yet, which is very different from somebody coming in week after week after week and saying, "I don't have anything to talk about. Life is going well." The most difficult plateaus for a therapist, which signal more an ending than a plateau, happen when the patient comes in and wants to convince the therapist of how well they're doing: "I'm good, you're good, everything is good." Therapy really ends whenever the curiosity has left the room for either the therapist or the patient. At that point we're going back over material, not in a way that is particularly fruitful, but just marking time.

---

If you've been in therapy for a longer period, you should have the sense that you're not interacting with exactly the same therapist as you were in the first weeks. The therapist should have learned something along the way; we would hope that you've influenced them just as they've influenced you. As we get to know patients well, and they come to know us, there's a shorthand that develops, there's a history, and it's part of the relationship that really equips you to move forward. That's something you should be able to expect as you move through the relationship. Notice whether your therapist is growing in this relationship with you. If that's not happening, it may be time to leave.

There's another, perhaps surprising, reason it might be time to leave— it could be that you're getting too comfortable. Sometimes we joke that as soon as you get to the point where you want to stay in therapy, you need to start thinking about leaving. Good therapy is a very safe space, and in fact it can start to feel *too* safe. You may start to feel very secure in therapy. Maybe you're developing real inner peace, a way of being at home with your therapist and then at home with yourself. Giving that up can feel risky. It's normal to actually cherish it.

But the goal is to take that inner peace, that being at home with yourself, out into the world, much like a child eventually leaves their family.

Kirk has had a patient who's grew so comfortable in therapy that they seemed to have forsaken a social life. They built a relationship with him and with other members of a group in therapy, and that seemed to be where all their social energy went. But the goal of therapy is to take that energy out into the wider world and not confine it to therapy sessions.

Therapists have something in common with parents: It's our job to work ourselves out of a job. *Failure to launch* is a phenomenon we talk about when young adult children can't seem to leave home and make their way into the world. Failure to launch is a failure of both parent and child; neither one can change or break what has become a dependent relationship, whether the child depends too much on the parent, or the parent cannot let go. The same sort of dynamic can develop between therapist and patient. So if you get too comfortable, it's time to start asking some important questions of both your therapist and yourself.

But we've saved the best for last. The best and happiest reason to leave therapy is that you really have reached the point of getting everything you need from a therapeutic relationship. If you feel that way, congratulations! It's satisfying to arrive at a point where you feel equipped with the self-understanding, and recognition of the relationships that you need to better make your way through the world.

Life isn't easy, and it's your therapist's job to help you navigate its perils. If you've grown through this relationship to the point where you're ready to head out on your own, that means we've done our job.

Still, you may not quite be done. It's important to leave the therapeutic relationship well, so that you can really make the best of what you've learned. And you may feel the need to return periodically, just to check in about developments and how well things are going. We'll talk about those possibilities next.

CHAPTER 24

# How Can I End Therapy Well?

When it's time to move on from therapy, it can be hard to know how to approach it. In another chapter we addressed the question of needing to leave because it isn't going well. If you're in a situation where you're not being helped, we really do want to encourage you to speak frankly about it and know when to leave. But now we're talking about something different—ending a therapeutic relationship that has gone well, that has helped you.

We've heard several reasons from patients as to why they're ending therapy:

"The expense is starting to add up."

"I want to try doing this on my own, without your support."

"I've gotten everything I came for."

We're not writing this to judge your reason for deciding to leave. Rather, we want to talk about the process. *How* you end therapy is at least as important as *why* you end therapy. Still, understanding the reason is an important part of that process. We want to be sure it isn't just an impulsive decision triggered by something that happened in therapy that made you feel misunderstood, or that you're angry, or there's some other crisis you're not mentioning or even recognizing. We want to help you slow down and make a thoughtful decision rather than an impulsive one.

Whether you're ending it because you're unsatisfied or because you're completely satisfied, it's important to understand why. Is there something you're trying to escape? Is it simple discomfort with a strong feeling? We don't ask this as a way to keep you in therapy. The goal of therapy is to finish, to be equipped to live your life. We want to talk with patients about their reasons as a way of understanding how things have gone and how they're doing.

It's important to pay attention to how the thought of ending therapy makes you feel. What emotions does it elicit? Does it excite you? Does it bring a sense of relief? Or perhaps you may experience what the Portuguese call *saudade*, which is a feeling of bittersweet longing. Surprisingly, it is not uncommon for someone ending therapy to experience feelings of grief or loss. *Saudade* captures the feeling of love that remains after someone is gone. Walking away from someone you have told some of the most intimate details of your life and who has accompanied you on countless journeys of exploration can be painful. It is through therapy that we can learn to tolerate and grow from such losses. Sometimes we hear patients who are leaving say things that seem wistful:

"I don't talk to anybody else about these things."

"I am more myself with you than with others."

"I don't have anybody who listens to me the way you do."

It's important to ask what underlies such thoughts. What are they doing that's causing people not to listen to them? Why don't they have a sense that other people understand them? Is it that the world is so screwed up that nobody can understand them, or are they doing something that really *interferes* with people trying to understand them? Those kinds of things that people might say at the end of therapy are valuable for them to think through, to understand, to be curious about. Kirk often says there's a good chance that people end therapy in a way that's consistent with their personality. There's a good chance that you'll end therapy in the same way you end other relationships, and even a very good chance that you'll exit this world in a similar way. One of our patients said, "I see my ending as graduation." Kirk joked with him later, "That's the way I think you're going to go out of this world, you're graduating into something else." It seemed quite characteristic of everything Kirk had learned about him.

---

The biggest red flag for us when a patient wants to end therapy is abruptness. There are of course times that therapy has to end abruptly. Perhaps it's a sudden, dramatic change in life—a job transfer, a sudden long and serious illness. But those are more extraordinary circumstances. Usually, if somebody who has been in long-term therapy just leaves, it means something didn't go right and probably started a while ago. That's important to understand.

It's helpful to keep in mind throughout the therapeutic process that it will come to an end. Your therapist should periodically check in with you to see if your perceptions about the progress that you're making match theirs, and also to give you the opportunity, as therapy is unfolding, to step back and observe the process, to see what you've accomplished and what might yet be left to do. That way both patient and therapist can have a better sense of how things might be going—and whether therapy might be winding down.

Once patients have decided to leave therapy, we'd like to see them come back at least two or three times to bring their therapy to a conclusion. Again, this isn't a way to cling to patients; it's a way to make sure they're equipped for what comes next.

Sometimes in those last sessions, Richard will ask patients to project themselves forward six months and describe their life to him at that point: What's happening? How they are feeling about being out of therapy? How are they handling events that are coming up in their lives? Who are they talking to? Ask these questions as if they're living that life now, so it's in present-tense language. Richard asks them to imagine whether they have regrets about the way that they've left, and whether they have the tools that they thought they had when they left to do this. He might generate some of the questions, and then on the basis of their responses, they might end up generating some of their own.

In those last few sessions, we want to be candid about what we've seen, as we offer our personal reactions. We might give them the opportunity to ask any questions that they may have wanted to ask but have for one reason or another have not asked during treatment. We may not answer those questions if they're too personal, or if they seem like throwaway questions meant to incite something. But we want to answer as many questions in good faith as we can.

We will often tell people—if it's true—how much seeing them has meant to us, how much we've learned from them. It's a very candid, personal discussion. We're actually still trying to accomplish a lot, still exploring, right until the very end.

Frequently patients will ask whether they can come back. In fact, we do think it's a good idea to see them again six months or so later, just to check in and see how it's going. But they might want to return for longer, too. Sometimes patients are doing long-term work, not immediately rooted in a particular set of symptoms. Our response to that is usually that our door is always open. If you have a desire to return, something is going on. Call. We'll see if more therapy is helpful, or whether you might need to see somebody else, depending on the issues you're facing.

Yes, the ending to therapy must come. Your therapist knows that. But it's important to leave in a way that prepares you for what comes next and reflects and uses all the important things you've come to understand.

# PART THREE

# With a Little Help From Our Friends

# CHAPTER 25

# Targeting Treatments

Effective psychotherapy affects all human aspects of the patient—body, mind, emotions, thoughts, and behaviors. The focus may differ from one patient to the next and may change over the course of treatment. You may start out with *talk-therapy*, one-on-one with a therapist, in the context in which most of us think of therapy— in an office or online, talking about your problems or your patterns. It's a fairly straightforward pattern that has served many people well for generations.

But sometimes that *usual* way of doing therapy isn't enough. As you talk with your therapist, you or the therapist may begin to think you might benefit from something more, or something different.

An effective therapist will treat differently a patient whose primary concern is an addiction versus a patient whose primary concern is explosive anger. The therapist may develop yet another approach for a patient who may suffer from both. Fortunately, the field of psychology has developed many approaches, including some that are tailored for certain problems. Your therapist won't be trained in all of them; they're more likely to specialize in a single approach, or maybe a few. But they should be aware of all the possibilities and ready to refer you to one of them if appropriate.

In this next section we briefly present thirteen such specialized approaches. Each of the ensuing chapters have been penned by therapists who are colleagues of ours, therapists who we have worked with in group settings or individually. As you will see, some of these authors discuss their expertise and some of the approaches taken to treat specific kinds of issues or disorders. Psychotherapy, like so many other professional fields, can be very broad or very specialized.

We think that most people would be best served by beginning with the basic tools of talk-therapy. We don't recommend *starting* with one of these specialties, since we are convinced that the basic challenges address by all these different approaches have their roots in what you would address in basic talk-therapy. You may have questions about different specialties, and we hope we can at least begin to answer those questions here. But we would encourage you to rely on your therapist's expertise to answer the question of whether or when to apply a new approach. It's not unusual to pursue more than one track at once, for example, seeing a couples therapist while continuing with individual psychotherapy.

There are more than 400 different types of psychotherapy, so what we're presenting here is just a small sample of the various approaches you might find. Some are well known, such as couples therapy or grief counseling. Others are less so; you may learn here for the first time about *brainspotting*, or *EMDR*. And the final entry isn't so much about a single approach you're likely to find, but instead about the benefits of an interdisciplinary approach between doctors and therapists.

We hope that by familiarizing yourself with some of these different approaches, you will better understand the full range of what the field of psychotherapy can do to make your life better.

# CHAPTER 26

# Couples Psychotherapy

## By Kristin Kuiper, LMSW

*Love,* a sculpture by Ukrainian artist Alexander Milov, depicts two wireframe adults sitting with their backs to each other, defeated and distanced after a disagreement. Within these wireframe adults are two wooden figures of children faced toward one another, holding out their hands in an attempt to reach each other. This sculpture beautifully and truthfully illustrates something that unites us as humans. We enter the world with a commonality across cultures, races, and social groups—the innate need for connection and belonging. Along with pursuits of connection throughout life, first in one's family of origin and later in the context of intimate relationships, comes the inevitability of experiences that harbor disconnection, disharmony, and disorder.

Couples therapy focuses on the intimate relationship system created and held by two unique individuals. It provides a contained setting and opportunity for a couple to work on healing and growing in areas of struggle, and also to become more aware of the enduring vulnerabilities they each carry because of the relationship experiences they have had throughout their lives. In that sense, couples therapy can lead to both individual and relational healing and growth.

I have found it essential to be trained and become an expert in a specific model and approach to this work. Mainly because of its research and theoretical base, I chose to study and be trained in the Gottman Method, developed by John and Julie Gottman. As a Certified Gottman Therapist, I am equipped to comprehensively assess a couple's relationship, assist couples in skill development, help them repair past hurts, and improve connection in their relationship. The Gottman Method provides research-based concrete skills and tools for couples that help improve their friendship, manage conflict more effectively, and develop a sense of shared meaning together. It begins with a thorough assessment of the relationship and then a plan for treatment is established based on the needs of the relationship.

My particular approach as a couples therapist is integrative, combining the Gottmans' model and several other couples therapy approaches, theories, and techniques. My work with couples is driven by three relationship values—healing, authenticity, and growth. Also integrated into this approach is the relationship the couple develops with me as their therapist, one of respect, compassion, and generosity geared toward each partner's growth and flourishing within the relationship. I also model relationship skills in the dimensions of communication and emotional boundaries and normalize common relationship ups and downs.

My couples therapy approach is dyadic: I intervene in the couple's interactions while they are talking to each other, rather than having each partner talk to me while dispense advice and solutions. The goal is to have the couple change the way they interact so they can experience positive change in their relationship and improve how they experience life together.

A couple does not have to be in crisis to benefit from couples therapy. On average couples wait five to six years after the onset of a relationship problem to pursue help, which makes changing patterns and dynamics more challenging. Instead, I recommend viewing couples therapy as a resource, which promotes the happiness and stability of a relationship over time. This process can be productive whether a couple is targeting a specific relationship challenge (conflicts about money, for example), preparing for a milestone or transition (such as the birth of a baby), or confronting an experience of relationship upheaval (a breach of trust, a traumatic event, or an addiction). Couples who have *good* relationships can also benefit from therapy. They can learn how to deepen their friendship and intimacy and strengthen their emotional connection.

If there is violence in the relationship, I do not recommend couples therapy. Increased vulnerability and self-disclosure may result in physical or emotional harm, and safety is a core priority. If there is an active addiction, that can be cause to recommend delaying couples therapy until individual treatment and recovery is in process.

Couples recovery is a valuable and important part in individual addiction recovery; it's a simple matter of timing regarding when a couple is ready to begin couples work. If there is a current affair (not including polyamory or open marriage), I do not recommend couples therapy. Instead, I make specific recommendations to each partner and reviews options for moving forward.

An overarching goal of couples therapy is to help prevent the couple from needing to re-enter therapy for the same reasons that they initiated treatment. The treatment structure that supports this goal is called *massing and fading* of sessions.

At the beginning of couples therapy, sessions are regular and consistent, usually weekly for sixty or ninety minutes. As relationship gains are made and sustained, couples move to a biweekly and then monthly session frequency.

The length of active couples therapy can vary from six months to three or more years. As a couple transitions out of active couples therapy, continued sessions on a less frequent basis may occur with the purpose of troubleshooting challenges and reinforcing integration of the couples work. Some couples elect to have a monthly therapy session without a defined end to meeting, using therapy as a part of their relationship support structure.

Some typical interventions used in couples therapy include:

**Psychoeducation**: The couple learns research-based components that contribute to healthy, happy, and stable relationships.

**Relational skill building techniques and strategies**: Couples learn and practice specific skills and tools that help improve their friendship and intimacy, manage conflict effectively, and build a sense of shared meaning and purpose together.

**Mindful dialogue**: Structured dialogue with one another includes slowing down, assigning roles of speaker and listener to improve expression of self and the ability to listen non-defensively.

**Internal working model identification**: Identifying and increasing awareness about how present reactions or contributions to dynamics are rooted in each partner's personal history.

**Physiological regulation**: Skills of self-soothing, body sensation awareness, and mindfulness practices are integrated to assist each partner with emotional regulation.

**Boundary work**: Identifying who is responsible for what—feelings, opinions, attitudes, beliefs, and actions, and practicing taking responsibility for oneself.

One thing for you to know if you are contemplating couples work is that there are two perspectives for every set of facts—and both people are right. Often, couples want me to determine who is *right* and who is *wrong*. It takes practice to learn how to shift the focus onto the process of listening to understand and speaking to represent yourself well.

Imagine a *healing* version of the *Love* sculpture; the two wireframe adults turned toward one another, embracing, while the two children inside hold hands with relief and delight. As a couples therapist, I hold this vision for each relationship I work with as I facilitate the movement from disharmony to connection.

# CHAPTER 27

# Grief Counseling

## By Shelley Dennis, PhD, ABPP, HSP-P

Loss—and the resulting grief—is a universal, something everyone experiences at some point. And yet, we often avoid thinking about it because it can feel messy or out of control. I know that when I experienced my deepest loss thus far, I was completely paralyzed. That's embarrassing to admit; as a licensed clinical psychologist with over twenty years of experience, I've helped hundreds of people cope with their grief. And yet, when my world was suddenly thrown off its axis, I had no idea what to do.

What is grief, anyway? In her book, *The Grieving Brain*, neuroscientist Mary Frances O'Connor differentiates between *grief* and *grieving*:

> "[G]rief [is the] intense emotion that crashes over you like a wave, completely overwhelming, unable to be ignored. Grief is a moment that occurs over and over. However, these moments are distinct from what I call grieving, the word I use to refer to the process, not the moment of grief. Grieving has a trajectory. . . . Grief never ends. . . . You will experience pangs of grief forever. . . . Your grieving, your adaptation, changes the experience over time."

Those pangs never go away, but your reactions to them can change over time.

My psychological training did not prepare me for the moment I got the call that my father had died of a heart attack. It was utter devastation, like a wave had crashed over me, a building had collapsed on me, an avalanche had buried me. My grief about that moment is still the same, even years later.

That was the beginning of a string of losses, but not the end. Six people I considered close died within the next two years. Still floundering from my dad's loss, I felt each loss knock him down a rung on what felt like an already eternally long recovery ladder.

Then one day, as my siblings and I were sorting through my dad's things, I found a three-ring binder labeled *Quincy Street Consulting and Crafts.* Inside was a series of drawings, contracts, and legal paperwork related to an unrealized small-business dream. It was his *retirement* plan, turning his hobby of woodworking into a company named after the home he had built for his family over forty years ago. At first, I felt intense heartbreak when I realized what this represented. But then I began to feel inspiration. He ran out of time, but I am still here.

Probably the most well-known research in the field of grief and loss is attributed to Swiss American psychiatrist Elisabeth Kübler-Ross. Her extensive work with the dying led to the internationally bestselling book *On Death and Dying* in 1969, in which she proposed the five stages of grief as a pattern of adjustment: denial, anger, bargaining, depression, and acceptance. While Dr. Kübler-Ross's focus was on describing the experience of someone who was facing their own imminent death, bereavement experts have since used these five stages to describe the experience of that person's loved ones. However, I have found no formal program that offers step-by-step skills to take individuals through the process. Instead, I have focused on a series of grief exercises, which I call SMART Grief, in which individuals walk through the experience of grieving in a healthy way—in their own space, at their own pace. It can also be used by therapists to help patients navigate the grief process.

SMART grief tools focus on five main skills represented by the acronym SMART:

**Storytelling:** This is the first and most important skill in the set. To grieve something, you have to be able to describe what you're grieving. What happened? How did it make you feel? How did it change your life? Each of the five weeks contains an exercise to practice storytelling skills to help articulate the traumatic event in a healthy way.

**Mindfulness:** Working to develop emotional awareness, body awareness, and breath work is essential to staying grounded during the process. Learning the skills and then practicing them daily starts with this step.

**Action:** Research has demonstrated that behaviors like moving your body, going outside, participating in grief activities, and doing things that would likely bring positive feelings (e.g., having *fun* can be beneficial in dealing with grief.) This step focuses on bringing an action component to the grieving process.

**Relationships:** Connecting with others, accepting help, finding ways to give to others, and physical connection (e.g., hugs) can help with loneliness and emptiness. In addition, finding ways to set boundaries within relationships and identify your needs in relationships is an essential skill in grieving well.

**Today:** Getting through grief effectively requires day-to-day functioning. You have to keep going. And, while we hope that you have found a way to do this all along, this fifth skill helps clarify and potentially better organize how you spend your days. The focus is on setting up a schedule, integrating skills, and prioritizing a healthy lifestyle.

One thing Kirk wishes he had known before starting his own grief journey was that it would elicit both emotions and physical sensations in my body that I didn't like at all. For me, this included a lot of crying and so much fatigue. I also wish I would have known that grieving is not a linear process, and that I would have to go through several rounds of work to see progress. But the ultimate goal is to take it step-by-step and integrate these new skills into your routine. Ultimately, our grief can be the tool that connects us more deeply to those around us.

CHAPTER 28

# Group Therapy

## By Brian Ashtin, LCSW, LMSW, CGP

Modern group therapy has its origins in 1905, when internist William Platt found that his tuberculosis patients responded better when they were able to discuss his presentations on hygiene in discussion groups. Sharing of information and joining with others brought hope, a sense of belonging, and better health outcomes. This is still true today. Being in a group promotes healing and better health. In a sense, Platt was doing therapy in the group by imparting information that was important to their health, but the sense of community allowed the information to be better used.

Today, there are many methods to group therapy. As in Platt's case, there are groups in which the leader gives information, such as psychoeducation groups and skill-building groups. There are also groups in which the therapist does one-on-one therapy with each member in succession. In these groups, the others get the benefit of vicarious learning.

However, the kinds of groups that I want to discuss are the groups where the leader is less the agent of change but rather a facilitator for the group members to help one another grow. In these kind of groups, new knowledge about oneself and others and resolving interpersonal difficulties as well as symptoms such as anxiety and depression happens as a result of difficulties that emerge in a communal context. With the right guidance of the leader, group members become valuable to one another and aid in mutual growth.

Here's an example that illustrates many aspects of what are referred to as *psychodynamic* group therapy or interpersonal process groups. Ken, a thirty-five -year-old single male (a group member for about eighteen months), was seeking treatment because he felt unlikable, always sad, and lonely. He came into group one day and announced that it would be his last day in group. He had gotten a lot out of it, and felt grateful to others, but felt there was nothing more for him to gain.

People had a variety of responses. Some wished him well; another envied his progress and wondered when he would be ready to leave the group. A couple of others expressed polite sadness. Ken nodded to this and the group, including Ken, fell silent.

After about five minutes of group silence, I asked another group member, one who often feels left out, how Ken felt about the group's response to him. He said, "Probably pretty shitty. No one is asking him to stay. I bet his feelings are really hurt."

At this point, Ken angrily said, "Yeah, no one cares about me in this group. No cares if I live or die. You guys don't give a shit about me."

Realizing this statement encapsulated Ken's core pathogenic belief, I asked the group, "What's with you guys? How come no one cares if Ken lives or dies?"

Susan then spoke up. "Ken, do you really want to know why I haven't asked you to stay?" Ken nodded. "Every time I express some feelings of longing or disappointment toward someone else, you trot out your quasi-Buddhist bullshit about 'renouncing desire, non-grasping, yada, yada, yada,' and I won't keep getting hurt. It's you that's hurting me. I feel criticized by you, and I get the feeling you don't even want to try to understand me."

Another member said, "Me too. I feel criticized by you a lot. Who needs that? I get enough of that at home." Ken became quiet. I asked him what he thought about what Susan said. With tears in his eyes he said, "I feel like I don't belong here. I feel pretty unimportant and alone." Ken's old core injuries were rising to the surface, and everyone felt it.

Another member said, "I can see that. I haven't wanted to seem mean to you, so I've been avoiding you instead." Ken, now openly crying, began to say how lonely and unlikable he feels. His unconscious strategy of trying to compensate for this painful and self-destructive belief by offering advice in the hopes he would be seen as useful and likable was now out in the open. He painfully recounted the repeated experience of punishment and neglect at age seven he experienced when his mother died. His father was too overwhelmed himself to tolerate Ken's sadness and bewilderment.

Al, who is older than Ken, responded with warmth to Ken. With tears in his own eyes, Al told Ken of his own experience of neglect and loneliness. He said he really felt close to Ken right then and would have treated him differently if Ken were his son. Ken responded with the fantasy of being hugged and comforted by Al. Al said, "I would like that, too. I think it would feel very good to be close to you." It was a powerful moment of repair for Ken, in which he learned that his openness and vulnerability about his self-doubt would not drive others away.

Others responded warmly to Ken and expressed admiration for his vulnerability. He felt supported, cared about, nurtured, and seen. And the group therapy setting made that possible.

Of course, Ken was compelled to keep repeating this pattern many times, but the group was now able to ask him what the feeling was behind his giving advice. This led to his increasing ability to directly express the need for attention when he was feeling left out or alone in the group in ways that did not get others to recreate his early trauma.

---

There are many benefits to therapy in a group setting. One is that problems that may be hidden in individual therapy will emerge in the group. Another is that one gets to see that one's problems are not unique or shameful. Groups act as a hall of mirrors; one can see oneself in others, leading to greater self-awareness of guilt or shameful feelings. It is also an opportunity to gain self-esteem by being helpful to others, and to decrease the loneliness and isolation that is the cause for a lot of personal suffering. And when one observes others being courageous in the group, one can be encouraged to be brave, too. The group leader may help a member work on an issue or may help two people work something out together. They will also help group members understand their own roles in the group.

Regardless of the focus, the leader's goal is to help create a unique, safe environment where people can understand themselves, how they are perceived by others, and their tendencies within relationships—and thus to grow.

# CHAPTER 29

# Relational Psychodynamic Therapy (RPT)

## By Benjamin Reisterer, LPC, Certified Relational Psychodynamic Therapy (RPT)

The *relational turn* in psychodynamic therapy began to emerge and take shape back in the 1980s. At that time, the field began to focus on the idea of a *two-person psychology,* meaning that 1) there are two human beings with affect, emotions, histories, hopes, dreams, desires, and needs in the room, and 2) it isn't actually possible for the therapist to keep their own subjectivity out of the process. This allows the therapy to become truly dynamic, creating great potential for healing in an authentic encounter of the two people. This has been alluded to in the field from very early on. As Carl Jung wrote in 1933, "The meeting of two personalities is like the contact of two chemical substances: if there is any reaction, both are transformed. We should expect the doctor to have an influence on the patient in every effective psychic treatment, but this influence can only take place when he too is affected by the patient. You can exert no influence if you are not susceptible to influence."

Relational Psychodynamic Therapy, or RPT, views symptoms that bring people into therapy more as invitations to explore underlying core wounds, rather than something to be managed or eliminated. Symptoms are the messengers that let us know something needs tending to, rather than a problem in and of themselves. One analogy is that of weeds growing through cracks in concrete. You can find many ways to cut the weeds back, but if you don't get at their roots, they quickly reappear. You then repeatedly find yourself back where you began, which can become frustrating and exhausting.

Therapists, generally speaking, have worked hard to hide behind theories, interventions, and homework in order to avoid our own pain and discomfort (symptoms) in knowing that we can't actually *fix* anyone. We can only undo aloneness, relieve suffering, develop a better relationship with one's wounds, and help to bring more authenticity and vitality to life. We only have a chance at this by entering *into* suffering with our patients. Scottish psychiatrist Ian Suttie called it "a fellowship of suffering" to describe this act of sacrificial love—extending oneself for the sake of the other. This is ultimately the catalyst for what brings treatment to life and makes it effective. By being as vulnerable and compassionately authentic as we are asking our patients to be, our natural inborn processes for healing come online, offering a chance at a more fulfilling life. The goal is to seek to understand, with curiosity and humility, what roots our painful symptoms are attempting to invite us toward, and to courageously accept that invitation. While we do seek symptom reduction and/or remission, we do so by pursuing vitality in our patient's lives.To help us live with more authenticity and vitality, it is important to hold to the container of therapy in a specific way. We, as relational psychotherapists, commit to paying attention to the *there and then* (What happened in your story? How have you learned to adapt? How is it continuing to impact your life?) as well as the *here and now* (What is unfolding between us both in our experience of one another and how we interact?). Inevitably, we find a great deal of overlap between these two, so holding to the *here and now* allows both therapist and patient to engage the symptoms and adaptations developed in the *there and then* in real time, together. Essentially, we pay close attention to what is getting stirred in both of us—our emotions, memories, metaphors, and random associations. Then we work to courageously give voice to these in an invitational, curious, and exploratory way to begin to get at what is happening beneath the surface.

The idea of *intersubjectivity* or *intersubjective space* is a key concept. Essentially, the therapist is actively listening and attuning to their patient but also keeping their attention on their own affect and mind, their own raw organic material. The therapist turns it over in their mind, asking, "Why is this being stirred in me at this moment with this person? What is happening here?" When this happens, the subjectivity of the therapist and the subjectivity of the patient have met in the *intersubjective space* and are mixing together, creating something new. The aim is for this to go back and forth, sometimes being initiated by the therapist and sometimes by the patient. The more times that two humans authentically meet in this space, the more fertile ground is created for change.

As you can imagine, working this way can be terrifying. We are working to be as honest and authentic with one another as possible, which means that the reality of conflict, inherent in all human relationships, needs to be tended to and worked through. I do not mean that we fight or that we simply blurt out spontaneously what we feel, or become aggressive verbally or physically with one another, but that we strive to fully encounter one another without the need to force either of us to be different, to yield, to manipulate, to abandon, or to dominate. We hold to the tension and seek to continue to generously extend ourselves with curiosity to the *why and what* that is seeking to be worked through.

This is very different from how we tend to experience or engage with others in our day-to-day lives. Often our experience of others can be objectifying; things are fine as long as they are meeting needs or at least not causing the experience of difficult emotions. It is a real and rare gift to hold the space of the reality of what is *actually* being experienced, and to tend to that over what is simply socially acceptable. This is also the container where we can find ourselves being able to *work things through* instead of *acting them out*. We tend to have go-to patterns of relating or being in the world that are brought online by certain experiences or feelings to avoid discomfort or pain. Now there is a chance to grow the resilience of these experiences, but to also find a healthier and more life-giving way of engaging.

Moving through this process often leads us to the presence of deep grief—grief for our own wounds, those we love, loss, the world, endings, and more. These are incredibly painful yet unavoidable realities of being human and are therefore necessary and sacred. When we bring our grief outside of isolation and into the presence of another, or in community, as it is being experienced, we find great relief. We know that as we move forward, the marks, scars, strengths, and memories of the past make us more fully human and alive and able to enjoy what now is.

As we begin to find new and more authentic ways of being in the world, we mourn our old ways. We know we are becoming more vulnerable, which is scary and hard, but it is the way to a life of deep authenticity, connection, healing, and vitality.

## CHAPTER 30

# Meditation and Mindfulness in Psychotherapy

By April Kaiserlian, LMSW

*Mindfulness* and *mindfulness-based psychotherapy* are foundational practices and approaches that support cultivating moment-to-moment awareness of self as well as self in the context of others. They can also be applied to awareness of longstanding generational patterns. In fact, the contemplative practice of *mindfulness meditation* is a modern umbrella term that contains hundreds if not thousands of nuanced ways to approach the body and mind in the present. Due to the depth and variety of meditation practices and traditions, it is highly recommended, if not a requirement, that the clinician has their own meditation practice and does not offer meditation practices they themselves have not yet practiced.

When using meditative practices in the therapy space to cultivate moment-to-moment awareness, it is vitally important to understand the aim of the practice. Frequently, clients will report that meditation does not work for them, which is often due to an oversimplification and overgeneralization of the practice. As it stands, the majority of both clinicians and clients associate meditation solely by focusing on breathing.

Meditation practices can be loosely understood as falling into the three categories of practice—*steady, study,* and *shape*. The distinction between each category is porous. There is a flow and flavor of steady, study, and shape found each in the other.

**Steady:** Steadying is the most familiar aim of modern, secular meditation practices. Mindfulness is most strongly associated with the practice of focusing on the physical sensation of breathing as a means of concentrating one's attention in the present moment, and concentrating your attention on the present moment is the steadying aspect of meditation. People often report an increased experience of calm when they learn to steady their attention and live one moment at a time.

The steadying aspect of meditation can be practiced and strengthened through a variety of body-based practices such as focusing on the breath or a full or partial body scan, as well as movement practices such as walking, yoga, and tai chi. Steadying can also be practiced through word-based practices like a mantra or *single-word* practice, as well as lovingkindness and compassion practices.

**Study:** Studying is the aim of meditation practice that supports the cultivation of insight into one's moment-to-moment experiences as well as one's relationships and ever-changing environments. Meditation teacher Susan Kaiser Greenland once aptly said, "Mindfulness is becoming aware of one's inner experience and one's outer experience without confusing the two." Adding the aim of studying to the aim of steadying creates a challenging and interesting meditation practice. Meditation risks becoming dull or boring or viewed as selfish and naval gazing when the *studying* aspect is not included.

The studying aim of meditation is richly supported by meditating with a community and/or with a teacher or trained psychotherapist. It is often by studying oneself and bringing more mindful awareness to one's experience of the therapeutic dyad or group that one cultivates rich and ongoing insights related to self, and self in relationships.

Studying is also supported by using practices such as *noting* as a part of one's steadying practice. A foundational noting practice is to silently name the felt sense of one's changing experience in the body and mind as pleasant, unpleasant, or neutral. Noting can also be used to begin to name one's emotional experience. The *body-scan practice* is a body-centered practice of noticing the tone or tenor of sensations moment to moment.

Another modern and well-loved studying practice first developed by meditation teacher Michele McDonald and popularized by teacher and author Tara Brach is the RAIN practice— *recognize, allow, investigate*, and *non-identify and/or nurture*.

**Shape:** Shaping is the aim of meditation practice where the practice moves from a formal practice to an informal or *life-centered* practice. Shaping means a person begins to integrate and apply the insights gleaned from studying into one's daily life. The goal of shaping is to decrease reactivity and increase agency—especially in stressful moments. Shaping is characterized by an increase in wisdom and compassion as well as a deeper connection to self and others.

Shaping is a vital and necessary means *and* end of any meditation practice. The 2,500-year-old meditative tradition called Buddhism, as founded by the Buddha, is an elegant and incisive path that is dedicated to the end of suffering and the liberation of all living beings. Indeed, this aim is too large for any one person but is the intention that underlies all personal and collective moments of addressing stress.

When applied skillfully and with support, meditation practices have been shown to have a neutral-to-positive impact across most client populations. However, there has been a growing awareness and education about how to best offer meditation practices in a trauma-informed manner. In short, any meditation practice should be applied and practiced in a way that supports "distress tolerance" instead of distress overwhelm. The best trauma-informed approach is to stop any practice when self-connection or presence is compromised or to shift the steadying focus of the practice to a neutral or pleasant anchor in the present moment.

Mindfulness can be applied in two ways: explicitly, in the therapy dyad or group setting as one of many formal practices, or implicitly, as the clinician organically leads the client(s) into a more mindful and aware state, stepping out of the rhythms of normal life to become more aware of, and more intimate with, their present-moment experience. Meditation practices are best practiced with support, found through a trained teacher and/or psychotherapist or a local meditation community. And it can be used beyond therapy to become a lifelong practice.

# CHAPTER 31

# Specialized Gendered Therapy for Men

## By Randy Flood, MA, LLP

Authors' note: You may wonder why we cover specialized therapy for men, but not for women. The answer is simple: Men are often held back from seeking therapy by the traditional gender roles and expectations they have internalized, and as a result far fewer men enter therapy. Specialized gender therapy is intended to help men overcome those barriers.

While there is a fledgling contemporary ethos of gender fluidity, many males who seek counseling are influenced by more traditional expectations of societal norms. The enculturation and socialization of males can create unique and specific struggles in identity formation, relational deficiencies, and emotional intelligence. This presents specific challenges and barriers to the therapeutic process.

Males are often raised to believe that to be man enough, they must strive for independence, self-control, self-reliance, and rugged individualism. Accordingly, seeking therapy can be met with resistance since it runs counter to how males are taught to solve emotional problems, deal with relational struggles, and essentially make it in life. Engaging in counseling can seem *weak*, even though men regularly seek out help with improving everything from their golf swing to their financial portfolio. Men's therapy, or *Men's Work*, is a uniquely gendered approach to engaging males in a therapeutic process that too many men believe to be acceptable only for women.

Although general counseling can be helpful for men, I believe that the challenges inherent in initiating Men's Work are essentially best overcome in men's groups. It is in the men's group where males learn about the courage it takes to remove their masks or armor and reveal their more vulnerable inner lives with other men. The men's groups provide new clients with access to elders who can shepherd and help socialize them in the process of reclaiming and transforming the range of human emotions with which they were born. Then they can build an emotional intelligence that is both nimble and strong.

Male clients also learn the art of relational intimacy in these groups. The dual track of focusing on developing emotional and relational intelligences ultimately provides them the symptomatic relief they often seek when entering therapy for relationship problems, depression, lack of meaning/purpose, loneliness, anger problems, or other issues. Moreover, it provides a therapeutic resocialization process with other males, which cultivates their humanity while not sacrificing their masculinity. While male clients often approach counseling with the fear of being emasculated, they come to realize they are engaged in a kind of cross-training.

If a male client presents with an addiction, or what is called an externalization disorder—an acting out of unwanted feelings of fear, shame, or loneliness onto others—he is placed in a psychoeducation program incorporating individual and group sessions. These programs—anger management, substance use disorder, domestic abuse, sex/porn addiction, etc.—provide education, support, and accountability with other males who struggle similarly. Once a client successfully completes a psychoeducation program, he is invited to continue his healing and growth in a psychotherapy program.

While some male clients transfer into a psychotherapy program, others begin their counseling experience by participating in weekly individual and men's group psychotherapy sessions. This therapy group process provides powerful opportunities to heal shame and overcome fears. It offers healthy male-to-male relationships where clients can experience intimacy and human connection beyond the limitations of shallow banter or bellicose boasting. Male clients experience these groups as safe places to lay down the emotional wounds they've secretively carried for years. They build their strength in showing emotional courage through sharing their vulnerabilities with others. This fosters a more grounded and solid sense of self, which they then integrate into their relationships outside the group.

The men most ready for men's group work include:

- Male clients who have experienced injurious male socialization that impacts their beliefs and values about masculine identities, emotions, and relationships.
- Males who have had absent or abusive fathers in their lives and a general lack of positive male mentoring.
- Males who struggle with loneliness and self-esteem and use intimate/sexual relationships with women to buttress their emotional and relational insecurities.
- Males who carry around a lot of shame about being good enough, or man enough, yet hide their shame and insecurities with performance, work, and posturing.

Males who struggle with generalized aggression toward other males when triggered or challenged may not be appropriate for a group experience. They may need more prolonged individual therapy before they are ready to take this next step.

Some typical interventions used in Men's Work include:

**Psychoeducation** helps clients understand and appreciate the gendered male socialization process and the limits it places on developing their full humanity and human potential. By revisioning a healthy, more balanced masculinity, they can give themselves permission to do the inner work necessary to heal and grow.

**Somatic therapy** facilitates clients in reclaiming their body sensations and emotions. This enables them to have more self-awareness and greater capacity for intimacy with others.

**Role playing and psychodrama** allows clients in group therapy to re-experience buried emotional wounds and provides a corrective relational experience.

**Regressive but controlled anger work** allows clients to therapeutically express old anger that is being suppressed or acted out onto others.

**Compassionate dialogue with themselves and others** assists clients to better understand and appreciate the inner child survival strategies and patterns rooted in fear.

**Encouragement of personal disclosure** allows clients to experience the empathy of others, which reduces their shame.

Some cognitive/behavioral approaches are also utilized, which help clients develop healthy belief systems, coping mechanisms, and self-regulation strategies.

Males often pride themselves on demonstrating physical courage, such as the courage it takes to run into a burning building to save a life. But success in the twenty-first century demands that men possess more than physical and mental toughness. It requires them to be willing to evolve and grow and to seek wellness and balance in their lives. Men's work takes emotional and moral courage. It's akin to putting on your oxygen mask before saving someone else, which flight attendants encourage precisely because it's necessary. It's the kind of courage that might not change or even save just your life, but also the lives of those closest to you.

# CHAPTER 32

# Bodywork in Psychotherapy

## By Ronald J. Hook, LMSW, CGP

Neuroscientists have been realizing more and more that therapy is incomplete unless there is meaningful work with the body. The realization has emerged largely from the study of trauma and its dissociations. But dissociation from core emotions is a widespread condition. Most recently neuroscience has been exploring the neural path of *interoception*—body awareness, or the awareness of internal sensory processes that carry emotion up the body toward consciousness. This experiential path has always been the stuff of Radix bodywork.

Radix means *root* or *source*. It is a study of the life force in all of nature, and most notably in the human body. It is also a sensory education about emotional experience and discharge, whose principles were developed by Wilhelm Reich, MD, and refined by Charles R. Kelley, PhD., founder of the Radix Institute.

To give you some sense of how this specialized sensory education can be applied to psychotherapy, consider this: We are born fully emotionally expressive. The emotion originates in the core of the body and expresses itself outward toward the periphery with muscular gestures and coloration, as well as with full breathing. As we develop, we become forcibly engaged in the civilizing process. We are not to bite; we are discouraged from crying aloud; we are not to scream in public places; we are required to get along with our peers. By the time we get to school we are usually obedient little soldiers, physically inhibited enough to be trained in groups according to the standards of the civilization in which we live.

Along the way, we must learn to muscularly inhibit emerging emotions so that they do not offend our trainers, or our friends. Without always even realizing it, we begin holding our breath, averting our eyes, sticking the tongue into our nasal pharynx, closing our glottis, and tensing our diaphragm against a pending sob, a burst of anger, a belly laugh in an inappropriate place, and other unwelcome emotions. On both a subtle and grand level this process is going on with great frequency from late infancy to school age and beyond. Along the way it becomes unconscious, as the muscle movements involved become chronic patterns of tension.

The natural flow of emotional expression is longitudinal, basically from the abdomen upward through the face and eyes. It is easiest to see the path of a wild laugh or a deep sob. Anger moves up the back and forward through sharply focused eyes and sound. Fear moves suddenly upward and back with a sharp inhalation, sometimes including widening eyes and raised arms. Love, happiness, disappointment, pleasure, and pain all have their natural physical paths of expression. Generally, the softer feelings move expansively up, out, and forward, while painful and fearful experiences produce contraction and protection.

Suppressing muscles are arranged in seven known transverse layers, or segments. One is around the eyes and base of the skull; another is around and in the mouth; a third is in the neck and throat; a fourth and fifth are in the breathing muscles of the chest and diaphragm, and on down to the abdominal pelvic muscles.

One sample principle of Radix bodywork is to work first with muscle tensions around the eyes, always making sure they reflect presence—being in the *here and now*, not preoccupied or distracted—before working on the next segment below in the character armor. I spend time with this segment of the armor in nearly every session.

In regular psychotherapy we want the person in good contact with reality before exploring further emotion. In body-oriented work, presence in the eyes is the indicator. Is the gaze fixed? Do they seem preoccupied? Are they watchful? Are they allowing themselves to be seen? With this small sample of the eyes, one can begin to see physical parallels to the psychological defenses. Obviously, tensions are lodged in the muscles of the other segments as well.

When a person enters a session, I experience them as a constantly moving, pulsating organism. Of course, there are many pulsations in the body: breathing, the heartbeat, peristalsis, and on down into the cellular level. Sometimes I imagine the client as a nervous animal that has entered the room with me for the first time, hovering near the door. I try to be restful enough for them to eventually approach, even if that's only one step.

Initially, I will lay out what the work is about. I will let them know that it's a sensory education to help them be more in touch with their own body, and in the end, to give them options they may not have known they had. I do not want to change them. I may bring certain things to their attention, not to criticize them, but to increase self-awareness.

Once I have established contact and presence, I will guide them to look downward and inward, bringing their attention into their breathing, down into their legs and into their feet. They become aware, as gravity pulls them down through their feet, sensations are absorbed into the small nerves of the feet and are electrically carried up the longer nerves of the legs and spinal cord to the brain, of the experience of gravity's pressure. As gravity pulls downward, interoception moves upward. This becomes useful in guiding attention into various parts of the body, searching to permit that part of the body to send the sense of itself through the nervous system up to the brain.

Practicing various exercises while maintaining the breathing permits the muscular inhibitions unique to this person to come to the surface. As I observe these, I introduce various alternatives to help move the muscles in question. As a small example, someone may typically exhale through a tight throat, pinching the discharge of the air. With their permission I might stand close to their ear and give them an example of the sound of a gentle exhalation moving through a dilated throat. I'll ask them to hear the difference, to do it their way, and then to attempt to imitate my way. Few realize the control they have over their throat, and the way they breathe through it, much less formulate sound. The purpose isn't to train them to breathe like me; the purpose is to show them options. Besides, breathing through an open throat may help them access a desired level of power or vulnerability within their own body.

There are many interventions for the eyes, the facial muscles, the tongue and throat, the shoulders and back of the neck, frozen chests, tense diaphragms, and areas of the body. The practitioner needs to learn them carefully and apply them sensitively. Good, mentor-based training and considerable work with one's own body are essential.

While I believe the need for bodywork is universal in therapy, the specifics of a session depend on accurate assessment, accurate perception, and accurate intervention. There are methods that can be learned. Half of that learning is through work with one's own body, where a sensory recognition of the other makes its imprint. The other half is learning a coherent theory. And, of course, personal boundaries must be clear.

Radix work also includes building those boundaries and some conscious inhibitions, especially if the emotions flow too much. These interventions can help a person live a more disciplined and mature life.

Whether through helping the client open up or helping establish boundaries, Radix can help people live their lives with greater access to purpose and meaning.

CHAPTER 33

# Intensive Short-Term Dynamic Psychotherapy (ISTDP)

## By Laura Meeker Wicksall, LMSW

ISTDP is a psychoanalytic therapy developed by Habib Davanloo in the 1960s. Discouraged by the length of time that traditional analysis required, Davanloo set out to develop a more intensive and short-term therapy that could effectively treat patients, especially those patients who failed to be reached in traditional analysis. Davanloo found his model to be particularly effective in treating patients who suffered from severe anxiety and character disturbances—specifically patients with internal conflicts that generated anxiety and a host of unpleasant symptoms, such as obsessions, compulsions, depression, or relational difficulties.

Today, ISTDP falls under the umbrella of Experiential Dynamic Therapy and works experientially within David Malan's triangle of experience (included below). ISTDP therapists work rigorously and systematically with a patient's defense, anxiety, and affect (emotion) in the therapy session, which makes the therapy continuously experiential in practice.

Defense Anxiety

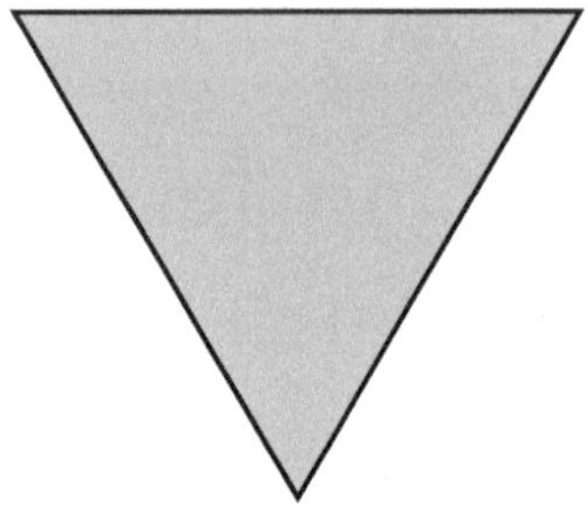

Core Affect

Patients who can most benefit from ISTDP are those patients who are very good at *sliding by* in traditional talk-therapy, without making progress that is of deep and lasting benefit. These are patients who present with good intellectual and cognitive insight but maintain an emotional detachment that disturbs their life and relationships. These patients have often participated in numerous psychotherapies but find themselves frustrated with the continuous symptoms of anxiety, depression, and relational disturbances they are desperate to change. These patients often unconsciously resist and sabotage their own treatment, hiding behind facades of compliance, detachment, self-criticism, defensive affects, and intellectualization that serve as a major barrier to their emotional health and authenticity.

Patients with relational challenges such as avoidance and/or fear around intimacy and emotional closeness can benefit from ISTDP. It is a relational therapy that focuses extensively on the therapist-patient relationship, bringing special attention to fears and anxiety that emerge, and working actively to address underlying feelings that drive these symptoms.

Patients that experience continuous distress related to anxiety are also great candidates for ISTDP. Because ISTDP focuses on anxiety as a symptom of unconscious conflict, the model is very successful in helping individuals address their internal conflicts, especially around emotions, which address the core of their anxiety and reduce symptoms.

ISTDP has a unique focus on the patient's defenses, which is why it is so effective in treating patients who are often resistant in traditional analysis or psychotherapy. Defensive systems are very complex, but examples of commonly used defenses include the following: intellectualizing, detaching, ruminating, smiling over affect, avoidance of affect, defensive affects (weepiness/reactive anger) eye avoidance, anxiety, vagueness, passivity, and indefinite speech. The purpose of focusing on defense/resistance is two-fold: 1) to make the patient more conscious of their resistance and the way it impacts their life and symptoms, and 2) to draw out unconscious conflicts and bring them to the surface. ISTDP therapists work systematically with defenses to clarify them, explore their origin, and current functions, as well as the consequences they pose to the patient. With the patient's willingness, the therapist begins to apply pressure on the patient to relinquish resistance and explore underlying feelings in the session. The patient begins to experience conflict between resistance and authenticity and overtime, can turn against defensive patterns, face their authentic feelings, and achieve greater connection and internal peace.

ISTDP has a systematic and sophisticated way of working with a patient's anxiety. Due to its intensive nature, ISTDP is an anxiety provoking therapy for patients. It is necessary to mobilize a patient's anxiety to stir up unconscious feelings and conflicts, and yet equally important to keep the patient within their window of tolerance. For this reason, a careful and continuous assessment of the patient's anxiety is crucial. Therapists conceptualize anxiety as a physical and physiological experience, thus making it easier to differentiate from defenses and core affect (emotion). ISTDP therapists are trained in understanding somatic pathways of anxiety and distinguishing those from somatic pathways of emotion. Therapists work with anxiety differently depending on how anxiety is discharged somatically and/or tolerated. Some patients easily become dysregulated and need assistance with anxiety management, while others have good anxiety management and can tolerate pressure and challenge in the therapy.

ISTDP has a strong focus on emotion and achieving emotional connection internally and within the therapy relationship. The model focuses on the somatic experiences of emotion and helps patients become familiar with the somatic pathways of their rage, pain, guilt, and sadness. Distinguishing somatic experiences of emotion from anxiety in the body and defenses is a very important aspect of ISTDP. This distinction helps patients remove defenses and anxiety, in service of a deeper connection with their emotional world. Emotion is treated as a very important gatekeeper to the unconscious, and through emotional connection patients can gain insight into the unconscious conflicts that lay at the root of their distressing symptoms.

Transference (focusing on the patient's feelings toward and with the therapist) is an important aspect of ISTDP and becomes a major focus of the therapy. When the therapist works closely with the patient's resistance it mobilizes the *complex transference feelings*, which are then explored in the therapy relationship. The transference feelings help the patient understand their deeper relational conflicts and repressed feelings toward family members, which frees the patient up from oppressive relational distress. The focus on the transference makes the therapy work very interactive in the patient/therapist relationship.

Here are some necessary requirements to participate in ISTDP therapy:

1. A willingness to be open and honest with one's feelings and experiences.
2. Engagement based upon one's own volition and desire (not mandated or coerced to participate by outside party).
3. Ability to identify a difficulty that is psychological in nature and internal (within self not caused by others).
4. A willingness to take an active role in one's therapy.

5. Youth and adolescents are not typically good candidates for ISTDP particularly if they are in environments in which their defensive mechanisms are still necessary and functional for them. Likewise, individuals who are in chronically traumatic and unsafe situations may also not be good candidates for ISDTP due to the necessity of resistance/defensive mechanisms for adaptation and psychological survival. Individuals with Borderline Personality Disorder may also not be good candidates, due to difficulty identifying and experiencing internal conflict.

CHAPTER 34

# Eye Movement Desensitization and Reprocessing Therapy

By Elizabeth Raese, PsyD

Eye Movement Desensitization and Reprocessing (EMDR) is a therapeutic approach that uses memories to access and shift stored meanings. These stored meanings from the past exist in the form of body sensations, sensory information, emotions, and beliefs, informing all our perceptions and experiences in the present. These associations occur automatically and most often below the level of our conscious awareness.

If you have ever had a time when you overreacted or had an emotional reaction that surprised you, this gives a clue that emotional learning from your past may have been activated. For example, during your annual review at work, your boss gives you many pieces of strongly positive feedback and makes one small comment about an area for improvement. While you know *rationally* that your boss values your work and you are good at your job, you *feel* a rush of shame and find yourself obsessing over this one comment. Some negative belief associated with past experiences, such as "I'm not good enough," shaped by repeated experiences of harsh disapproval from a parent in childhood, was awakened in this moment and amplified your reaction.

EMDR was originally developed as a trauma therapy. EMDR

makes sense to consider if you know addressing trauma is your goal for therapy; it may also make sense to consider if you don't identify with the word *trauma*, and are looking for therapy to help shift patterns in your emotions, thoughts, relationships, or behaviors.

I like the definition of trauma as something that is subjectively experienced as "too much too soon (or too fast), too much for too long, or too little for too long." There is an appreciation within EMDR that in addition to *big-T traumas* (e.g., being in a serious car accident or witnessing violent deaths in combat), all humans experience some *small-t* traumas, impactful experiences that contributed to the development of negative beliefs (for example, being threatened in third grade by a much larger fifth grader for months and feeling too scared to tell anyone). EMDR can be helpful with either.

There are many creative and effective ways of working with EMDR. It can be used to develop greater access to strengths and positive beliefs. It can also be used to help you prepare to face an upcoming challenging situation. While it is important to be aware of the flexibility of how EMDR can be used, the focus in this introduction to EMDR will be on its use with reprocessing memories.

To begin reprocessing, you and your therapist will select a memory, a specific moment in time that you experienced as distressing or overwhelming. By asking some specific questions, your therapist will help you identify and connect with beliefs, emotions, and body sensations associated with this memory. Once the memory is activated, bilateral stimulation is used to help your nervous system reprocess the memory. Bilateral stimulation is sensory stimulation that alternates between the left and right sides of the body, such as following a light side-to-side with your eyes, hearing a sound move from the left ear to the right ear, and/or holding buzzers that vibrate in the left hand and then the right hand. Between "sets" (periods of tracking the light, feeling the buzzers, and/or listening to the sound alternating between your ears), your therapist will check in with you about your experience and make any adjustments needed, such as changing the duration of the sets or the speed of the movement of the light. If any intense emotions or sensations arise, your therapist will be present to offer support, perspective, resources, and connection to help you in these moments.

EMDR gives structure to this experience, yet within this frame, there is room for tremendous flexibility. Part of what can make EMDR so fascinating and so effective is how the experience of reprocessing is highly individualized to your nervous system. Some people experience EMDR as a richly visual experience, seeing images and sometimes receiving new insights in the form of metaphorical pictures; others report feeling physical sensations moving through the body or noticing strong emotional shifts. For some, the experience is subtler, and they may even question whether it is helping. The process of EMDR has ways of assessing this over time, and it is not uncommon for people to experience notable benefits even if their experience of reprocessing is not as dramatic in the moment.

Reprocessing a memory allows the past experience to link to current adaptive information. For example, after reprocessing a memory of a life-threatening experience, a person is able to connect (not just in a logical way, but rather in a deep *felt* sense) with the knowledge of being safe now. EMDR trusts that with the right conditions, your nervous system will know how to do this.

There isn't a right way to do EMDR, so your experience will be your own. Showing up with openness and being able to relax expectations about what "should" happen will offer the most room for a helpful experience.

Just like with any other type of therapy, whatever your go-to strategies are for coping with stress or painful emotions, you can expect those will show up at times during EMDR. Having an attuned relationship with a therapist you trust will make a big difference in being able to recognize and navigate these moments. Creating an environment and relationship of safety and trust within which you can learn more about your emotional patterns, coping styles, and internal strengths and resources is fundamental to EMDR. This takes time.

Before reprocessing past memories, it is important that you and your therapist both feel confident that you have developed the relationship and resources to help you surf any intense waves of sensation and emotion that may arise. For the first experience with reprocessing a memory, it can be helpful to choose waters with gentler waves (for example, working with a recent experience of irritation, such as a frustrating interaction with customer service) to give you an initial feel for the process of EMDR.

Through reprocessing past memories associated with negative beliefs, people describe experiencing more freedom, confidence, and clarity in the present. People commonly express amazement that memories that have haunted them for decades no longer hold an emotional charge. EMDR uses a scale of 0–10 to assess emotional disturbance associated with a memory. After starting EMDR with a memory rated 10, I have heard many people comment at the end of reprocessing and reaching a 0, "I *never* thought that it would be possible for this memory to be a zero."

People who are highly cognitively oriented (with limited access to or awareness of emotions and body sensations), individuals with pervasive or intense trauma histories dating back to childhood, people experiencing patterns of high-risk behaviors or current safety concerns, and/or those with more intense dissociative symptoms will benefit from a slow and sensitive approach within EMDR. This typically means more preparation and more development within the therapeutic relationship before reprocessing memories with EMDR. EMDR requires access to evidence and experiences that can support more positive beliefs. If these are not sufficiently present, they will need to be further developed through therapy and life experiences before EMDR will be helpful. If you try EMDR and don't experience it as helpful after repeated reprocessing sessions working with a past memory, it probably doesn't make sense to keep doing this part of EMDR—though, of course, there is nuance to this, and it is important to discuss your experience with your therapist. It may be that more preparation and experiences to support new positive beliefs are needed before resuming reprocessing, or it may be that another therapeutic approach is a better fit for you at this time.

The length of treatment with EMDR can vary greatly depending on your goals, the depth and persistence of your internalized negative beliefs, and your current access to information and experiences that can disconfirm those negative beliefs. For example, if you have had a rich history of positive experiences and beliefs and then experience a serious car accident, the duration of EMDR may be as short as a few sessions before you notice major symptom reduction. In contrast, if you experienced abuse all throughout your childhood from your caregivers and had very few positive, supportive experiences in relationships, EMDR treatment may be expected to extend over years. One of the ways EMDR can be misrepresented is by overly characterizing it as a brief therapy with rapid results. While this can be the case, like any other effective trauma treatment approach, it cannot be rushed.

Unlike many types of traditional talk-therapy, EMDR is an experiential approach that doesn't need to rely heavily on words. If you have trouble finding words to describe your experiences or have found that despite repeatedly talking about experiences, your old patterns and messages haven't really changed, EMDR could offer another way.

CHAPTER 35

# Cognitive Behavior Therapy and Dialectical Behavior Therapy

By Aaron George, LMSW, CAACD

Cognitive behavioral therapy (CBT) is a popular form of psychological treatment that attempts to address problematic thinking and learned problematic behaviors. It is based on the principle that psychological problems can be treated through learning more effective ways of living and coping with problematic behaviors, which will then reduce patients' emotional suffering.

In CBT it is common for the therapist to focus on helping the patient identify distortions in their thinking that are creating problems in their lives and then help them to better attend to reality. This usually involves establishing a better understanding of the patterns that lead to these behaviors as well as the development of improved problem-solving skills, learning to calm the mind and body, and facing fears rather than avoiding them. A common therapeutic strategy for helping with interpersonal problems is the use of role playing to practice more effective interactions.

CBT is oriented to helping the patient change their thinking and behaviors and thus produce emotional changes that will enhance their calmness and stability. The therapist works with the patient in a collaborative way to develop an understanding of their problems and to create treatment strategies. Exercises in the sessions and *homework* are designed to promote therapeutic goals and improve coping skills. The therapist will focus primarily on what is going on in the patient's current life rather than focusing on what has led to their current struggles. Because much of the emphasis is on behavioral change, research is more easily tied to the outcome and effectiveness of the treatment strategies.

Dialectical Behavior Therapy (DBT) evolved out of CBT, building on its principles but expanding resources and approaches. DBT teaches distress tolerance, mindfulness, and safety skills, whereas CBT does not. DBT also emphasizes reality acceptance and emotional acceptance, rather than attempting to change emotions by restructuring thoughts, as CBT does.

The two therapies share a focus on connections among thoughts, feelings, and behaviors; the importance of homework and regular check-ins; and the high value of the client-therapist relationship.

Because DBT is less well known, it will be helpful to walk through how an experienced therapist has applied the principles of DBT to his own life and work as a therapist.

---

Marsha Linehan's breakthrough approach of Dialectical Behavior Therapy evolved from CBT in the late 1980s, focused on helping the most emotionally dysregulated find safety and a life worth living through a highly structured, team-based protocol. Clients learn techniques to regulate emotions and navigate crises, avoiding self-injurious behavior, by practicing skills in four core domains: Mindfulness, Interpersonal Effectiveness, Distress Tolerance, and Emotional Regulation.

Therapists are guided by Linehan's *DBT Skills Training Manual,* the framework's bible. The skills are taught to and practiced by clients from the *DBT Skills Training Handouts and Worksheets* book, which is provided to each participant at the outset of treatment.

DBT is intended to unfold in four stages. Stage 1 targets life-threatening behaviors such as cutting. Stage 2 addresses problematic emotional, behavioral, and cognitive patterns. Stage 3 focuses on problems in living, such as challenges with self-esteem, relationships, and goal achievement. Stage 4 is about the pursuit of a more meaningful life. In practice, that progress rarely occurs in linear fashion, but the design is still instructive.

I joined a formal DBT program at my organization in 2015, with about ten other therapists. We met for weekly group consultations that began with a different member facilitating mindfulness exercises each week, as rules stipulate that clinicians must practice the same skills they are teaching to clients. From there, we would present cases, problem solve, challenge each other to uphold the protocols.

Clients were required to sign a twelve-month-participation contract, given the high dropout rates among the target population. This stipulated their participation in weekly skills training in a group or individual format, weekly one-on-one therapy, and after-hours skills coaching by phone with their individual DBT therapist. Individual therapists were sometimes the person's skills therapist, but sometimes not.

There was a level of comfort in sharing responsibility for these demanding clients, a hopefulness that the well-researched scaffolding could sustain their complex needs. It was messy and inconsistent, but many participants experienced wins, however individually defined: Less cutting; saying *no* to a family member; daring to begin a new relationship. Those achievements seemed improbable without the help of the program. My experience led me to conclude that DBT can be a good thing, even lifesaving, for many persons, particularly those with borderline personalities.

Still, aspects of the program are draconian, particularly the rule to withhold contact with clients for twenty-four hours after they self-harm. The rules are in place for good reason, but DBT is not necessarily for the faint of heart. I didn't consider myself faint of heart, but I was left yearning for more flexible ways to help clients. So after a year as a therapist in a formal DBT program, I left for an outpatient position with another organization.

Several years later I opened my own outpatient practice, where I occasionally encountered clients who, at least on the surface, seemed like those I might have encountered in the DBT program. One in particular was occupying significant mental space. She self-harmed routinely and severely, requiring multiple inpatient hospitalizations during her first few months with me.

Thankfully, I had recently joined a consultation group composed of gifted outpatient therapists. It didn't take long for them to uncover my frightened, defensive posture, rooted in DBT programming, to target the cutting first and foremost.

A few minutes into my presentation, a colleague posed a critical question: "When are you going to start having a relationship with your client instead of with her symptoms?" My initial reaction was to dig in my heels, defend myself, defend my work with the client. But the question served its intended purpose. It helped me recognize that my laser focus on self-harm, while understandable, was a barrier between me and the person sitting on the couch.

Following that consult, I shifted gently from a primarily behavioral approach toward a behavioral-relational hybrid. My client noticed the difference; *I* noticed a difference. Empathy rose on both sides; therapy became lighter, less of a burden, something we often looked forward to. The question shifted my perspective from the problem to the person. The *relationship* now offered stability to buttress her in times of severe emotional distress.

Still, this isn't fan fiction. Years of pain and trauma didn't disappear overnight. The severity of my client's self-harm intensified due to online bullying and family conflict. While I was able to offer meaningful emotional safety, I lacked the time and resources necessary to secure her physical safety. She needed skills to forestall self-injury and suicide. She needed a higher level of care, so I referred her to a residential DBT program. Alas, it ended up not being the right setting for her, and after some contentious episodes that highlighted the limits of DBT's rigidity, eventually she left the facility. I don't blame the program or its staff, and I don't blame my client or myself. All parties had attempted to help her recover.

The client's experience coupled with my time in the program have taught me that DBT may be the right fit for many, perhaps the majority, of those with Borderline Personality Disorder. But there could be others who find that it exacerbates emotional dysregulation and prompts, rather than curtails, self-injurious behavior.

I've also concluded that neurodivergent clients may be likely to struggle in formal DBT settings. This includes those with Autism Spectrum Disorder traits and so-called maladaptive overcontrol problems stemming from severe anxiety. Clients with these characteristics often benefit most from a flexible approach. And *I* benefit from exercising patience, understanding, and awareness of my frustration and control urges when expectations aren't met, or direct verbal communication fails.

Neurodivergent traits may be easily mistaken as willfulness by a DBT therapist. And for a framework that emphasizes validation as a means of shaping behaviors, DBT's rigidity may, ironically, invalidate neurodivergent clients and diminish the therapist's influence on behaviors. The difficulty for persons in this category to engage in group activities, coupled with their sensory reactivity, underscore the need for proper assessment and for augmenting treatment to include one-on-one options.

CHAPTER 36

# Brainspotting

## By Rachel Duhon, LPC

Brainspotting harnesses the power of the brain to heal from the inside out, utilizing the attuned relationship between therapist and client to support the natural healing capacities of the brain and body. Your eyes are made up of brain matter and connect directly with the subcortex. The subcortex, or as we call it in the brainspotting community, "the land of no words," is nestled in the back of your brain, housing your emotional center, linking to your spinal cord and nervous system. Because brainspotting uses your visual field, it is bypassing the brain's *logic* centers and taps directly into the emotional center of the brain.

When you are in session and identifying the topic you'd like to address, there are many aspects of the experience that may enter your awareness, such as strong emotions, body sensations, repeating phrases, or mental images. Brainspotting refers to this as *focused activation.* As you are experiencing this focused activation, your eyes are reflexively and intuitively looking at specific spots in your visual field. Your eyes, looking outward, are accessing the specific spot in your visual field that is connected to the specific neuronal network in your brain that is associated with that particular topic. This phenomenon with your eyes is known as a *brainspot*—activity in the subcortex in response to focused activation and eye position. Keeping your eyes on these specific brainspots allows you to access the emotional energy that is trapped in the land of no words, making it possible for your body to do now what it could not do then—fully release unresolved emotionally charged experiences.

We are constantly brainspotting, but it is such a natural experience that we don't even recognize it in ourselves and in others. Try this simple exercise. Ask someone in your life these three questions and observe as they respond:

1) How old were you when you started riding a bike without training wheels?

2) Do you remember the name of your first closest friend?

3) What was the make and model of your first vehicle?

You will most likely notice patterns in their responses. Their eyes will move around quickly to find the answer to each question, slowing down or stopping to re-engage socially once the answer is found. If they cannot remember, you may notice their eyes continuing to move around, seemingly searching for the answer.

Here's what this looks like in a session. Every brainspotting session is unique, but there is a general framework that is used. You are asked to notice experiences and memories connected with the issues that have brought you to therapy. Your therapist will look for activation as you are tuning in to these experiences. Activation can be described as emotions, thoughts, memories, and/or physical sensations—muscle tightness, headache, heart racing, throat closing, etc. A common question used to help you identify your activation is, "What are you noticing in your body right now?" The therapist may also ask questions to assist you in identifying the location and nature of the physical sensations, which we call *body activation.* Bringing the body activation into conscious awareness facilitates deep brain (subcortical) processing and reduces the typical top brain (neocortical) processing to which we are accustomed.

Once we have the body activation, your therapist will guide you, either with your natural gaze or with the use of a pointer, to the specific spot in the room where you feel or notice the body activation the most. This spot will give you the greatest access to the subconscious land-of-no-words capsule, where the emotional issues or content is stored. From there, your therapist will invite you to engage in focused mindfulness, processing, noticing, and following what comes up inside of you, whether that's physical sensations, emotions, or memories. There is no need to try and keep your focus on one event or issue. Your only aim is to keep noticing what is inside of you and follow *what comes next,* staying curious about your experience. By keeping your gaze on that specific spot, you have opened the capsule that holds all the experiences that are tied together.

To explain this in more detail, let's use the analogy of a computer. On your computer, you have folders. Each folder has a name, which we can think of as a category or theme. In each folder, there are multiple documents, all with different stories, but connected under the folder with the same theme. Organizing this way helps you to later find where your content is stored. The processes of your brain work similarly so you can learn, adapt, and survive efficiently. This is what your brain does with unresolved energetically charged material. When you are processing, the brainspot connects you to the specific folder (theme). Staying on that spot allows your brain to open and process every single document that has been connected to that particular theme, in ways that only your brain knows. In the land of no words, your brain does not process chronologically, or even with a beginning, middle, or end. Every file is opened and your brain moves between all of them. This is why we do not need to stay focused on a single event or feeling.

Everyone experiences brainspotting in sessions differently. Some people talk to share new connections or experiences coming into their awareness, while others process in complete silence. Some other common experiences include temporary changes in physical functions (heart rate, breathing, digestion, temperature, etc.) or sensory awareness (vision, sense of time, etc.). Your therapist will hold space for you in whatever way you need. Because you are accessing material from the land of no words, your therapist will be fairly quiet during your process, as attempting to give insight, feedback, or engage in dialogue will pull you out of the land of no words and bring you into your neocortex (where language is). This interrupts your deep subconscious processing and gets in the way of your body's innate wisdom and capacity for healing. Your therapist might ask, "What are you noticing?" "Where are you now?" or invite you to "Dive all the way into that." Responding to questions is optional and is advised only if it facilitates your processing.

Your therapist will manage the time for you, typically giving you a cue toward the end of the session with gentle prompts that begin the process of coming back into neocortical (top down) processing and moving away from the brainspot. After the brainspotting processing time, space will be provided for you to share, based on what seems important to you. Your therapist may also engage in a grounding or breathing exercise, to help bring your body fully back to the present. It's important to know that just because you moved away from the brainspot in session, that does not mean that your brain has stopped processing. You can expect to continue processing for two or three days after a session. Just like in-session processing, the ways that people experience post-session processing is unique. You may notice changes in energy, memory, dreams, emotions, or sensations. All of this is normal and will work its way through to resolution. Your therapist will work with you to ensure that you are supported in your experience of brainspotting sessions, both in and out of sessions.

Brainspotting can benefit anyone. It is a highly effective treatment for all ages, and can be done with individuals, couples, or groups in a range of settings. Brainspotting can be used to address a variety of issues including, but not limited to trauma, grief, mood disorders, ADHD, phobias, OCD, substance abuse, somatic issues (chronic pain, sexual concerns, etc.), eating disorders, attachment disorders, and performance issues.

Many people experience relief after one brainspotting session. Since brainspotting works at a deeply subcortical level, and because many of the issues and concerns we experience are complex and interrelated, it might take a few days, weeks, or months for you to become aware of the healing that is happening. Longer term issues, such as developmental trauma or substance abuse may need more time.

Brainspotting is something we naturally do, so it isn't overly complicated. Utilizing your brain and body's innate wisdom and healing capacity; brainspotting rapidly focuses on the core experiences, beliefs, and issues underlying your concerns, making this approach effective for long-term healing.

# CHAPTER 37

# Trauma, Pain, and Multidisciplinary Treatment

By Jim Rossi, PhD and Andrew Lewandoski, DO

Within our current healthcare system, pain often isn't treated holistically. Instead, physical pain and psychological pain are seen as separate entities and therefore treated by entirely separate kinds of providers. In other words, mental healthcare and medical healthcare often exist in silos.

Clinical medicine rarely applies certain central tenants of psychology, even though they seem obviously useful: validation of lived experience (I believe you), patient-centered approach (you know your experience best), holistic or systems thinking (you work as a unified whole; all the systems/processes in your body are interconnected), and serving as a partner in pursuing patient empowerment over functionally limiting symptoms (how can I help you achieve *your* goals?). And, in turn, while clinical psychology will often acknowledge physical conditions and may offer some symptom management techniques, physical symptoms are often largely seen as out-of-scope. Neither clinical medicine nor clinical psychology make an explicit connection between physical stressors and psychosocial stressors.

Yet despite our different practices, we have found that the patients that we (and others) historically have the hardest time treating are those with chronic pain accompanied by psychosocial trauma. Given this overlap in approach and population, we began to ask, "What if we worked collaboratively by sharing patients?" This experiment has transformed how we provide care, and more importantly, it has transformed the lives of some of our patients.

At the most basic level, *all* pain (both physical and psychological) is a subjective experience. This statement does not diminish pain; rather, the appreciation of this fact actually inextricably *links* lived experience and pain. Often, those living with chronic pain have either a high level of perceived stress or have lived experience consistent with trauma. In our minds, this differentiation is neither clear-cut nor necessary. Non-traumatic chronic pain (i.e., uncomfortable symptoms that are persistent and that are not caused by an acute physical trauma, like a car accident) quite often will be associated with psychosocial trauma or high perceived stress and involve multiple organ systems. Given this, any individual experiencing non-traumatic chronic pain could be aided by therapy. There are often multiple disparate, seemingly unrelated symptoms that can in fact represent a common underlying cause. And it's only possible to begin to understand that underlying cause by gathering context about a patient's lived experience and by understanding and treating interrelated things, like chronic pain and high perceived stress, concurrently and collaboratively.

At this point, you may find yourself incredulously asking *why?* Why isn't pain approached holistically and collaboratively when it makes so much sense to do so? The answer to this question is complicated and deserves its own entire chapter, but to keep it brief, our current healthcare system is structured to treat well-understood acute conditions (e.g., a heart attack). Providers get paid for what they do (fee-for-service), and there's not a model to get paid for time spent thinking critically, which is integral to treating complex, poorly understood chronic conditions. And finally, non-health states are approached from a disease focus rather than an individual focus. In other words, the current system is built to classify psychological distress or chronic pain into specific diagnostic labels and treatment protocols.

One of the major differences in our approach is that we are primarily interested in the root causes, called *etiology*, of patient suffering or pain. We want to know *how* a patient got to where they are, and we don't care as much about *what* to diagnose or call their experience. Because the healthcare system uses the same kind of framework for identifying acute and well-defined conditions (the aforementioned heart attack) as it does for nebulous and poorly defined ones (chronic pain), patients often get told that nothing is wrong because they don't meet specific diagnostic criteria despite immense personal suffering. This happens both in medical specialties, like rheumatology, and in psychiatry. When an individual's pain and lived experience gets dismissed, and often dismissed repeatedly, there are dire consequences for their emotional and physical health. Patients who are told there's nothing wrong end up feeling, then, like there must be something wrong *with them*. Approaching distress from an etiological standpoint ensures that the individual living with chronic pain and psychological symptoms is treated, rather than being turned away due to not meeting specific diagnostic criteria.

We both believe the patient knows more about their life than we do. Practitioners must humbly learn about lived experiences to best decrease suffering. Guiding an individual through their lived experiences and drawing connections between seemingly disparate issues (like migratory joint pain, abdominal pain, and depression) allows for an empowered patient walking the path toward health rather than a dejected sufferer who has been repeatedly told *they're fine* despite their own lived sensations. And what we're beginning to see anecdotally is that, when we take this approach and we collaboratively treat our shared patients, patient symptoms that would be considered to be totally separate in our current medical system actually improve *across the board*.

We refer patients to each other, and we collaborate on their care. This creates a community of care in which patients receive continuous validating care focused on increasing their functional abilities, both physical and psychological. Patient encounters aren't single occurrences. This isn't a magical, one-time fix. It's a positive feedback loop, a back-and-forth journey where improvement along any line lays the groundwork for further improvement. It is, perhaps, the opposite of the cycle that so many of our shared patients are used to experiencing— bouncing from specialist to specialist, having their experience and sensations questioned or dismissed, and being told there's nothing that can be done for them. Operating alone would reduce our effectiveness immensely, and it's this increased effectiveness that we're seeing beginning to transform the lives of some of our patients. We outline below what our patients get from seeing the other and identify what patients seem to benefit most.

When Jim's patients see Andrew, they get a corrective emotional experience. It's hard to underscore how important this is. Jim estimates that about 90 percent of his patients with psychosocial trauma have had invalidating experiences with healthcare providers. Andrew often provides corrective experiences for these patients; this *is* a psychological intervention in and of itself. Patients are heard and their lived experience is trusted. This can be corrective not just for previous medical system trauma, but can extend to other formational traumas like parental trauma, etc. Patients benefit from Andrew's deep knowledge of disease states and his honest approach to limitations and possibilities. Finally, and maybe for the first time, patients feel a sense of community that there *are* trusted providers that care about them and that work together to help them reduce pain/physiological discomfort.

The patients who benefit the most from seeing Andrew are those who have a history of chronic pain and one, or more, of the following:

- a history of small-*t* or capital-*T* psychosocial trauma
- executive dysfunction (ADHD, etc.)
- GI symptoms (IBS, UC, etc.)
- a history of invalidation within the medical system (frequent

healthcare contact without clear direction, poor outcomes with respective specialists, etc.)

When Andrew's chronic pain patients see Jim, they get treated with empathy, curiosity, and respect. They receive trauma-informed care with its inherent focus on lived experience. While Jim uses diagnostic tools and practices evidence-based care, there is less in-session focus on meeting diagnostic criteria or receiving a diagnosis. Instead, patients get a therapist who operates *relationally* first. Jim has a deep knowledge of psychotherapeutic interventions ( techniques like prolonged exposure), but he doesn't use them in a heavy-handed way. Rather, patients have the agency to choose when/how/if they want to engage in an intervention. Together, Jim and his patients thoroughly discuss and explore a given intervention's benefits and risks within the context of their trusted relationship before proceeding.

The patients who get the most out of seeing Jim are those who:

- are willing to engage with therapy
- are open to learning about perceived stress and PINE (the psycho-neuro-endocrino-immunology network, basically a network of communication pathways in the body that links environmental stress to chronic medical and mental health conditions)
- trust Andrew and trust his referrals. Patients walk into the first therapy session from a place of increased trust instead of skepticism, and that can really set the tone for a transformational experience.

Individual lived experience is inherently unique, and as such, is hard to capture in a standardized way. And yet, it needs to be standardized to be able to be systematically applied in the healthcare context. We are working together to create standardized tools that focus on capturing individual lived experience that can be clinically applied in any setting (rheumatology, primary care, therapy, etc.). We hope to make this work widely available to care providers in recognition that, for care to change, a system-level sea change is required.

That said, the need for system-level change doesn't mean individual patients are powerless. We'd like to share some tips for how to seek better care, but with a big caveat; there are often significant barriers to finding the right care fit—insurance issues or lack of coverage, specialist shortages and access issues, finite resources (time, energy, *money*), etc. Frustratingly, many patients have very limited choices or no choices at all. We acknowledge that these recommendations are simply not accessible to everyone.

A few tips to seeking better care:

- At the end of an appointment with any care provider, ask yourself "How do I feel when I meet with them? How do I feel when I leave their office?" If your answer is that you feel crummy, that you didn't feel heard, or that you felt erased or dismissed, consider trying to find a new provider if you can.
- When looking for a therapist, the most important thing is to find good rapport. How do you get along with this person? Do you feel comfortable with them (even if the topics of discussion make you feel uncomfortable)? Do you trust them? Do you feel like they trust you? Is it easy to talk to them? If not, try finding a different therapist if you can.
- When looking for a therapist, seek out someone who practices trauma-informed care (EMDR, IFS, etc.). Trauma-informed care is different from standard talk-therapy and can help address the root causes of suffering. Patients should also ensure that, before engaging in specific interventions, the therapist can talk about the risks and benefits of these techniques and be open to *not* using them.

- When seeing a medical specialist, listen to see if they say things like "I don't know" or "I'm not sure." The ability to acknowledge uncertainty is a sign that they may be more likely to work collaboratively with you.
- If something feels off about a first specialist opinion and you have the ability to seek a second opinion, we encourage you to do so.

Because you're reading this book, you're likely navigating or evaluating what it would mean to work with a therapist for yourself or someone close to you. If you could take away just one thing from what we've written here, we hope it's simply that the pain you are experiencing *is* real. It's real no matter what previous or current care providers may have said. We leave you with a small mantra that's accessible no matter your situation: *I can trust myself. I can trust my experiences.* This trust is the first tiny step toward empowerment, and empowered patients can begin to walk the path toward health.

# CONCLUSION

# Therapy is a Relationship

We've said this a number of different times in this book, but it's important enough to leave with you as the last word: The decision to enter therapy is a decision to enter a *relationship*. And it's absolutely vital that you approach it that way. Therapy has to be a relationship, or it simply won't work.

Real, authentic human relationship has been neglected in some ways over the last few decades. The pandemic significantly altered our habits of being in contact with other people, but even before that, the whole notion of relationship was under stress. In 2000 Robert Putnam published *Bowling Alone*, a groundbreaking study that shows just how disconnected we've become. Participation in everything from bowling leagues (the reference in Putnam's title) to religious services has been in decline. And social media can foster a false or limited sense of connection. We're able to know so much about each other, but the real and sometimes messy work of being in relationship has suffered.

But if you're going to heal emotionally, we're convinced that you simply have to do so in relationship. Why? Because in most cases, relationship is the source of the problem.

Yes, there are emotional conditions that are physiological in origin, at least as far as we understand. For example, manic depressive illness, or what we now call bipolar disorder, we recognize as something that needs to be treated with medication. That is, there's something biological, physical, in that disorder. We see the same thing in schizophrenia. People used to blame schizophrenia on mothers, but now we understand that different patterns of mothering are not to blame. We now see that it doesn't appear to be intrinsic in nature. It always happens at a certain age when the brain is transitioning from being able to have many deep fantasies to begin to distinguish between fantasy and reality. (See, not everything is about your mother!)

Nevertheless, so many of the emotional problems humans struggle with are located in relationships, often from the earliest ages. So that which generates the initial difficulties developmentally ends up being played out in various symptoms and various attachment styles; and it is through the relationship with the therapist that those factors from early on get played out in a very present way. Attachment is so central to how we develop. If we have a parent who wants us to seem perfect, that's how we're going to grow up in life—with significant focus on looking right, being right, acting right, and with not much room for doing things wrong. On the other hand, a parent who wants the child to try different things and not be afraid to fail will help shape a person very differently. Do you resolve conflicts by fighting, or submitting, or withdrawing? Those things get established so early and are so central to the human experience. And they have a huge impact on how you live right now.

Your relationship to a parent or parents is just the first of many relationships in your life, and over time, those relationships form a series of experiences that you carry with you into each new relationship. Sigmund Freud called that *transference*, and it simply means that any time you interact with someone, there are clusters of people you have internalized there with you from your past. If, for example, you say something to someone that's mildly sarcastic and they explode, the chances are that it's not what you said, but what they heard, which was likely informed by something they always heard in a previous relationship. But that's the kind of interaction your therapist is trained to understand and help you with. A good therapeutic relationship is one in which you can be yourself and explore just who and what else you're bringing with you along the way.

When Freud identified the idea of transference, that was the first model of describing how therapy is relational. The way patients lived in the world, their previous experiences of relationships, they'd bring in and transfer to the therapist. So if the way they learned to live in the world was to do what's right or to do what pleases other people, that's what they'd bring in and transfer in the therapist's office. So that's why it's a natural thing for therapy to be relational.

Some of the most formative things we learn, we don't learn intellectually; we learn them with our bodies. That's the only thing we can use to take in all this information, up until the time we can talk and understand language. In those critical months of our lives we learn with our bodies; that creates what Alice Miller, in her book *The Drama of the Gifted Child*, describes as a kind of prison that we live in until we get to a point in therapy where we can begin to melt down some of those walls so that the authentic self that got suppressed or exaggerated finally gets room to have more expression. That gets worked out, at least to some degree, in this kind of experimenting relationship with a therapist.

Obviously, for that relationship to work, it has to feel safe; it has to be dependable. But it shouldn't become a *dependent* relationship. What's the difference between *dependable* and *dependent*? If the therapeutic relationship is dependable, it means you can count on your therapist to be steady—to show up on time, engage in a cooperative way, pay attention, end the hour on time, all those reliable behaviors. You need to be able to depend on that structure to help both contain the emotions and provide the direction for more internal, deeper work. A dependent relationship, on the other hand, can be infantilizing, so that the therapist doesn't ask tough questions or challenge you. And the dependence can go both ways; it's also the therapist who can be dependent on the patient to meet their own narcissistic needs, or financial needs, or other kinds of needs. In other words, you need a partner in this therapeutic relationship who can be strong without being infantilizing, so that you can explore safely and are encouraged to explore fully.

When you're free and safe to do that exploring, what are you looking for? In the end, what therapy is about is the *truth*. Therapy should be a process of discovering the truth, hearing the truth, and speaking the truth—about your thoughts, your feelings, and your relationships. We humans get nervous about truth-telling; we refer to *our truth* because that's a way of keeping a defense around what we believe about ourselves. But it's therapy's job to get you from worrying about *your truth* to talking about *the* truth.

Finally, that's what this is all about. In the last few decades people have come to embrace this notion of *authenticity*—of the importance of being one's authentic self. That might feel like a modern invention, but it's not. Because authenticity is really simply a matter of telling the truth about who you are—to yourself and to those around you. Telling the truth is a timeless virtue, across cultures, philosophies, and religious traditions. And it isn't just a virtue. It is a way, finally, of knowing who you are, and being at peace with who you are.

Because there is no peace quite like the peace of knowing, and being at peace, with the truth. And that's why we believe so deeply in the healing power of therapy.